UNACCUSTOMED MERCY

SOLDIER-POETS

OF THE VIETNAM WAR

D1617539

UNACCUSTOMED MERCY
SOLDIER-POETS
OF THE VIETNAM WAR

Edited by

W. D. Ehrhart

TEXAS TECH UNIVERSITY PRESS

1989

This book was set in 10 on 12 Times Roman and printed on acid-free paper that meets the guidelines for permanence and durability of the Committee on Production Guidelines for Book Longevity of the Council on Library Resources.

Printed in the United States of America

Library of Congress Cataloging in Publication Data

Unaccustomed mercy : soldier-poets of the Vietnam War / edited by
  W. D. Ehrhart.
    p.   cm.
  Bibliography: p.
  ISBN 0-89672-189-2 : $12.95. — ISBN 0-89672-190-6 (pbk.) : $9.95
  1. Vietnamese Conflict, 1961-1975—Poetry. 2. American
poetry—20th century. 3. Soldiers' writings, American. 4. War
poetry, American.   I. Ehrhart, W. D. (William Daniel), 1948-
PS595.V5U53 1989

811'.54'080358—dc19   88-38693
                                                          CIP

Cover and jacket design by Patricia Barrows Maines

Texas Tech University Press
Lubbock, Texas 79409-1037 U.S.A.

ACKNOWLEDGMENTS

All poems appear by permission of the respective authors unless otherwise indicated.

JOHN BALABAN. "The Guard at the Binh Thuy Bridge," "Along the Mekong," "Mau Than," and "The Dragonfish" reprinted from *After Our War*, John Balaban, University of Pittsburgh Press, 1974. "Thoughts before Dawn" first appeared in *Carrying the Darkness*, W. D. Ehrhart, ed., Avon Books, 1985. "Mr. Giai's Poem" first appeared in *TriQuarterly*. "Words for My Daughter" first appeared in *Ploughshares*. All other poems reprinted from *Blue Mountain*, copyright 1982 by John Balaban, by permission of Unicorn Press, P.O. Box 3307, Greensboro, NC 27402.

JAN BARRY. "Green Hell, Green Death," "Floating Petals" and "Nights in Nha Trang," *Winning Hearts and Minds*, Jan Barry, Basil T. Paquet, and Larry Rottmann, eds., 1st Casualty Press, 1972. "Harvest Moon," *Demilitarized Zones*, Jan Barry and W. D. Ehrhart, eds., East River Anthology, 1976. "In the Footsteps of Genghis Khan," *Veterans Day*, Jan Barry, Samisdat, 1982. "A Nun in Ninh Hoa," *War Baby*, Jan Barry, Samisdat, 1983.

D. F. BROWN. "Vietnamization" first appeared in *Colorado Review* under the title "Sonnet." All other poems reprinted from *Returning Fire*, D. F. Brown, San Francisco State University Press, 1984.

MICHAEL CASEY. All poems reprinted from *Obscenities*, Michael Casey, copyright 1972 by Yale University Press.

HORACE COLEMAN. "A Downed Black Pilot Learns How to Fly," *Giant Talk*, Quincy Troupe and Rainer Schulte, eds., Vintage Books, 1975. "A Black Soldier Remembers," "Remembrance of Things Past," and "OK Corral East/Brothers in the Nam," *Between a Rock & a Hard Place*, Horace Coleman, BkMk Press, 1977. "Night Flare Drop, Tan Son Nhut," and "In Ca Mau," *Speak Easy, Speak Free*, Antar S. K. Mberi and Cosmo Pieterse, eds., International Publishers, 1977.

W. D. EHRHART. "The Blizzard of Sixty-Six" reprinted from *The Outer Banks & Other Poems*, W. D. Ehrhart, Adastra Press, 1984. "Twice Betrayed" reprinted from *Winter Bells*, W.D. Ehrhart, Adastra Press, 1988. All other poems reprinted from *To Those Who Have Gone Home Tired: New & Selected Poems*, W. D. Ehrhart, Thunder's Mouth Press, 1984.

BRYAN ALEC FLOYD. All poems reprinted from *The Long War Dead*, Bryan Alec Floyd, The Permanent Press, 1983.

YUSEF KOMUNYAKAA. All poems reprinted from *Dien Cai Dau*, Yusef Komunyakaa, Wesleyan University Press, 1988.

GERALD MCCARTHY. "The Hooded Legion" first appeared in *TriQuarterly*. All other poems reprinted from *War Story*, Gerald McCarthy, The Crossing Press, 1977.

WALTER MCDONALD. "The Winter before the War" first appeared in *Aura* under the title "At Lake MacBride." "For Kelly, *Missing in Action*" first appeared in *College English*; reprinted by permission of the National Council of Teachers of English. "Faraway Places" first appeared in *Ball State University Forum*. "The Retired Pilot to Himself" first appeared in *Poet Lore*. "The Food Pickers of Saigon" first appeared in *TriQuarterly*. "New Guy" first appeared in *Event* (Canada). "Caliban in Blue," "For Harper, *Killed in Action*," "Interview with a Guy Named Fawkes, U.S. Army," and "Rocket Attack" are reprinted from *Caliban in Blue*, Walter McDonald, Texas Tech University Press, 1976. "Once You've Been to War" is

PREFACE

The war poetry of the western world begins, of course, with *The Iliad*, in which Hector expresses the warrior's creed: "I have trained myself always, like a good soldier, to take my place in the front line and win glory." As he leaves for an overseas duty assignment, Hector prays to Zeus:

> Grant that this boy of mine may be, like me,
> preeminent in Troy; as strong and brave as I; a
> mighty king of Ilium. May people say when he comes
> back from battle, "Here is a better man than his
> father." Let him bring home the blood-stained
> armour of the enemy he has killed, and make his
> mother happy.
>
> (*Iliad*, Penguin, 129)

How utterly foreign these thoughts would have seemed to a young draftee after a month in Vietnam, no doubt a man whose image of war had been formed not by Homer or Virgil (he'd never been required to read them) or even by the significant war poetry of Whitman or Stephen Vincent Benet—but instead only by the silver screen: Hollywood. James Crumley, novelist and Vietnam War veteran, has identified the source of the average American's attitude toward war: "millions of comic books and B-movies." Other than in Crumley's novel, *One to Count Cadence*, if there is any mention of Homer or Virgil in the hundreds of novels and the thousands of poems written about Americans in the Vietnam War, I have not found it—yet to those who know the tradition of war poetry and who also served in Vietnam, the difference between Achilles and Hector and John Wayne and Gary Cooper is not really significant. They're basically, archetypally, the same.

One doubts, though, even as late as 1968 when Wayne starred in Robin Moore's *The Green Berets*, that anyone realized how completely this 2000-year-old heroic tradition was to become obscured by the reality of war in Vietnam.

Poetry usually propagates and perpetuates myth. Therefore, such disparate American war epics as Joel Barlow's *Columbiad* and Benet's *John Brown's Body* depend upon classic roots and archetypes, as does even Peter Bowman's *Beach Red* (1945), a moving verse novel about World War II. In epics, however, one loses sight of the carnage and horror in favor of the overall fated grandeur of it all; and in these and most of the other earlier war poems (Hardy's "Channel Firing," Arnold's "Dover Beach," Jarrell's "The Death of The Ball Turret Gunner," and Owen's "Arms and The Boy" come immediately to mind) the inevitable clash of tragic forces seems to hold a reader's primary attention.

That archetypal interplay was what many of us were taught to see in poetry and was no doubt what traditional poets, despite their respective levels of combat experience, were also conditioned to see and write about.

The war in Vietnam changed all that, too, and as a result the poetry which has come from this conflict is as different from the tradition as the war itself was from any previous one. Even in the longer poetic works such as McAvoy Layne's *How Audie Murphy Died in Vietnam* (1973) or Dick Shea's *Vietnam Simply* (1967), the whole becomes lost in the parts, and there seems to be no cosmic interplay at all, just the momentary lyrical thoughts of poets who see nothing but that day, that moment, that fire fight, who feel that perhaps nothing will ever be, nor ever has been, quite the same.

What has resulted is a different kind of serious poetry about the Vietnam War that has yet to find an appreciative audience, and I think the fault may be ours—the academics—who seem to have trouble assigning or anthologizing poetry that something can't be "said" about. In the sixties and seventies, the same problem initially obtained with the beat and black poets. With only a few exceptions, for instance, the poems in this collection are essentially non-"literary"; that is, they require little explication; they come from no recognizable tradition; they usually invent their own forms; and their only context is that of the rice paddy, the landing zone, or the jungle. In this light, I would urge that teachers and readers of this poetry learn the facts of the Vietnam War, understand the new metaphors and jargon of the GI, consult maps to identify the frequent geographical allusions, put aside their preconceptions about the war and what they think good poetry has been, and look at how fine these poems can be. In all cases, Vietnam War poetry speaks for itself, often in brutal, explicit language. After all, to those of us who served in Vietnam, the war was the most explicit experience we have ever seen, and not to use the language of the war would be to lie about it—and to be dishonest, even for the sake of art, is the one thing an American Vietnam War veteran is never going to be able to do. He feels that he has been deceived enough, and he refuses to inflict another lie on others.

What are these poems about? There is only one really universal subject: the *lack* of universals—country, God, truth, peace, even love. A few of the Vietnam War poets such as Balaban, McDonald, Komunakaa, and Weigl do see beyond the war to cyclical but not archetypal patterns of human existence; however, the majority of poets present only the now—the immediacy of the war that they feel has matured them abruptly beyond their years. Their subjects are taken from virtually all aspects of the war: fire fights; the jungle; Vietnamese children; rape; death of a buddy; body bags; the wounded; a rocket attack; black dudes in a bar; whores; old and young Vietnamese; street scenes; arrival in Vietnam; coming home; guilt; loss of innocence; trauma; memories; temples; Vietnamese markets; and so on—a veritable tapestry of the Vietnam experience.

Interestingly, in this anthology there are no political poems; those were written for the most part by the non-participants, by established poets such as Ferlinghetti and Stafford and Bly and Levertov whose anti-war poems helped define early on the intellectual community's opposition to the war. There is included only one love poem spoken by a soldier about his wife, and only McDonald's excruciatingly passionate poems about his family as well as Balaban's sense of history place real frameworks around the actuality of being at war in Vietnam.

Some of these men are too consciously writing "poetry"; others seem trying only to tell it the way they think it was by means of short lines. Some use *personae*, to varying degrees of success. Many use metaphor, but few do so consciously and consistently, and there are many lines that will make a conventional critic cringe. Some poets, however, have created mighty lines that stand among the best. In short, the styles and techniques are as varied as were the experiences of the war itself.

The themes of these poems range from the standard to the particularly modern. There are, of course, poems about the brutality of war; the loss of innocence; the unneeded death of civilians; and the sad actuality of a war that will never seem over. A few, such as John Balaban (the only poet of the war who speaks Vietnamese), imply a rebirth after the ravages of war. Most of the standard war themes are here. Virgil would recognize them: *arma virumque cano*, with the emphasis on man.

Making this body of poetry unique, however, are the new themes that reflect not only the war but the consciousness of the 1960s and 1970s in the United States. One should note that of the twelve poets in this anthology, ten had their primary experience with Vietnam during 1967-70, the years in which the American attitudes toward the war changed so radically. Until the North Vietnamese Tet offensive of early 1968, most Americans saw the war as winnable; but after the Kent State shootings of May 1970, few aware Americans sought any other solution but withdrawal. Little wonder then, that so much of this Vietnam War poetry shows disillusion and loss.

Consequently, the new (and representative) themes that are seen in these poems are as follows: the individual's sense of guilt because of his participation in the war; extreme bitterness at having been forced into the war; the essential stupidity and causelessness of the war; an intense feeling of dislocation, of being a stranger in a strange land; and over and over again, the theme of the ignorance of normal Americans, both overseas and at home. Overall, a reader senses that each of these poets feels used, hardly a cog in a mighty machine but rather a misfit, one who understands what no other American can.

As with their use of metaphor, these poets also use imagery in an eclectic manner, but greens (for the jungle) and black (as an ominous symbol) predominate, as does cold, an oddity unless one has been in Southeast Asia and realizes that historically hell has possessed the opposite qualities of one's mortal, geographical existence.

Many of the poems are dateable, and I should like to repeat my earlier suggestion that the best way to apprehend these works is to know their context. If for the Vietnam combat soldier the John Wayne myth died in a barrage of AK-47 fire, so for the Vietnam War poets did The New Criticism also lose relevance. The poetry of this war *must* be read with history and politics in mind; only then will the full intensity of some of these remarkable poems come through.

Overall, these poems are the products of men who were either raised or imagined themselves in Hector's image, as portrayed unknowingly by John Wayne, and who arrived in Vietnam ready to take their places "in the front line and win glory." Their poetry shows, however, how quickly their concerns shifted, as W. D. Ehrhart puts it, only to "the next step./The next step./The next step."

THE POETS

JOHN BALABAN's poems contain some of the richest and most sustained metaphors of all and should be noted for their sound and rhythms. Balaban alone seems able to refine himself out of his poetry and to become at times the Yeatsian smiling poet (one suspects an intentional "Lapis Lazuli" echo at the end of "Mr. Giai's Poem"). Able to transcend the immediacy of war, Balaban shows the basic unity of existence, despite man's brutal attempts to alter it. In "April 30, 1975," for instance, even though the Vietnam War has ended, there is still violence of yet another kind in Brooklyn. Nevertheless, the "dust of life" can (one hopes) be washed away by a "Clear Mind." Also, perhaps showing his maturity, Balaban is the only poet who writes of the role of poetry in "For Mrs. Cam, . . ."—and his poems do indeed "coat" themselves "in lacquers of the mind."

JAN BARRY's poems are marked by his bitter sense of irony, from the American soldier who replaces Ghengis Khan's "Ah so!" with "Gawd! Damn!" to the father's definition of a patriot:

> Well, I guess, a person
> who loves the land.
> Although some people act as if
>
> a patriot's a man
> who hates another land.

Reflecting Barry's 1962-63 service in Vietnam, his poems show the incredulity of normal Americans at the feeling of being in the green jungle or observing a Buddhist suicide by fire. (Here, as noted earlier, a reader should know about the protest suicides that led to President Ngo Dinh Diem's overthrow in 1963.) Barry's poems are basically realistic, repertorial vignettes that show innocent Americans being made aware of realities they have difficulty comprehending.

D. F. BROWN presents a bitter, apocalyptic vision in poems that are impressionistic and often stylized. Rimbaud's influence goes far beyond the epigraphs to "Returning Fire" and "Eating the Forest," and the opening lines of "Illumination" where the day has "a lime glow" and "evening lasts five gray minutes" capture the essence of being under the Asian triple canopy. In "Eating the Forest," "the 10,000 versions/of the war are one/in the great, late All-Night," and in most of his poems, the darkness of reality seems indistinguishable from the blackness of his nightmares. Sometimes, Brown's abrupt juxtapositions, as in "Returning Fire," create such a sense of disjointedness that even Gary Cooper would be unable to resolve it. Obsessed with green memories, Brown searches "for sunlight/through/this tangle" that has been this war.

MICHAEL CASEY's short-lined story poems are among the most cynical in this collection; and his basic view is that Americans who have been made to "feel strange" ("For the Old Man") are those who also brutalize the Vietnamese landscape ("A Bummer"), then consider a dismembered body only another "Road Hazard." His are illumination rounds of poems: short, sharp, clear, and didactic. When a reader realizes that every election in South Vietnam was either rigged or disallowed by the ruling junta of the time, the irony of the Vietnamese girl's having voted for "Hoa Binh" (peace) becomes supreme as the speaker, the American at war, says, "I did too."

HORACE COLEMAN, better than any other Vietnam War poet, presents in his "OK Corral East/Brothers in the Nam" the ironic juxtaposition of the American Frontier and the black American's newly enraged consciousness. Using an allusive compression unusual in Vietnam War poems, Coleman portrays accurately and omi-nously the black/white confrontation that pervaded the '60s, showing that this war within the war may have transcended the obvious shooting hostilities. Black/white imagery controls many of his poems: "The dark/like the VC always comes back"; "black fingers on our white throats"—and even though Coleman, like Balaban, presents a cyclical view of existence as in "In Cau Mau," the future is usually ominous and essentially terrifying. Finally, the poem "Night Flare Drop, Tan Son Nhut," must be read in context: the scene is Saigon (the main U.S. Air Force Base) and the date is January 1968 when the North Vietnamese unleashed their nation-wide attacks during what had been the annual agreed-upon truce period.

W. D. EHRHART, for many reasons considered the Dean of Vietnam War poets, shows over and over again the effect of the war on a youthful, aware consciousness. With the possible exception of Bruce Weigl and Gerald McCarthy, Ehrhart more than any other poet writes of the inability of an American to shed his feelings of betrayal and guilt that participation in the war engendered. Ehrhart's is poetry of statement; his lyrics are really little narratives of disillusion that move from a rather objective view that both sides cause destruction ("Farmer Nguyen," an early poem) to the bitterness of "A Relative Thing" where America seems to be the only villain. Most of his poems are intensely personal, so much so that one can hear him pleading for forgiveness ("Letter") or agonizing about his own image in Asia ("Making The Children Behave"). Emotionally a pacifist, Ehrhart does show in his major poem "A Confirmation," some measure of resolution and affirmation, but his poetry is best characterized by the ending of "The Blizzard of Sixty-Six" where despite everything, "the snow keeps falling."

BRYAN ALEC FLOYD's individual portraits of U.S. Marines are unique in the canon of Vietnam War poetry and remind one of Edgar Lee Masters' *Spoon River Anthology*. Often discursive, his poems startle the reader with adroit images: a maimed girl's expression of love *"strafes"* Sgt. Just's ears; and sound: PFC Morgenstein "had chosen the goal of his groin/and it was to grieve"; and the memory of kissing his wife makes PFC Morgenstein recall that "a piece of the sun/was in her mouth." Brutally descriptive one moment, lyrically lovely the next, Floyd's poems offer an ironic panorama of many different characters and attitudes. "Private First Class Brooks Morgenstein, U.S.M.C." is quite simply the best Vietnam War poem written about the love of a combat soldier for his wife, and the image of a uniform clinging to "him like a huge wet sock" aptly shows what it felt like to be an American in an Asian jungle.

YUSEF KOMUNYAKAA did not start writing poetry about Vietnam, but an encounter in graduate school with another veteran, who insisted that he must do so, may have sparked what has become an increasingly significant body of work. Unlike many of the other poets, Komunyakaa writes not only of individual experiences but also of groups: GIs on the beach, Viet Cong prisoners, Vietnamese after the fall of Saigon, the boat people. His images are often wrenching: a moon "cuts through/night trees like a circular saw"; alleys are littered "like the insides/kicked out of pillows"; boat people's faces resemble "yellow sea grapes." Most of Komunyakaa's poems show the measured reflection of a consciousness that is still expanding and is not limited only to the poet's own Vietnam experience as a black man in combat.

GERALD MCCARTHY projects two distinct sensibilities: the poet of "War Story" who writes brutal, jarring verse; and the later, reflective observer who, unable to force the war out of his consciousness, feels only an overwhelming coldness around him. His "War Story" poems are much like those of McAvoy Layne's *How Audie Murphy Died in Vietnam*: realistic, sardonic, image-free, immediate. "The Sound of Guns," however, and "The Fall of Danang" (set in the mid-seventies, seven years after his Vietnam service) show McCarthy attempting to achieve resolution, but failing. "The Hooded Legion" is the only poem in this collection about the Vietnam Wall, the Washington memorial, and is one of the few poems of the many I have seen about the Wall that is not (albeit honestly) sentimental. "Weaponless and cold" (McCarthy's main metaphor), Vietnam veterans in this poem wish for the impossible: a hand that could many years before have turned them aside.

WALTER MCDONALD is the most prolific poet in this collection and is one of the best poets writing in America today. McDonald is a literary as well as a personal poet, but like _Robert Frost (McDonald has been called "the Frost of Texas hardscrabble"), he never lets his personal anguish about the Vietnam War obscure his basic love of humanity. He selects a subject and universalizes it. He plays with tetrameters in one poem, then soars with free verse in the next. Above all, he writes of human relations, especially of family, and his sardonically allusive "Caliban in Blue" should delight anyone who knows Coleridge and Browning. Like Coleridge, McDonald's primary concern is with the "moral sense," and even though (in "New Guy") the American hears Vietnamese women speaking in "alien voices/like angels speaking in tongues," one realizes that the basis of McDonald's vision is a love of, and return to, the humanity that really counts.

BASIL T. PAQUET wants his readers to share his anguish at the deaths of men he tended as a medic—and he succeeds. Of all the writers in this collection, he seems most able to make his poetry recreate the uselessness of combat death, and his poems hurt. Although Paquet writes occasionally in *persona*, a reader knows that it is Paquet himself who has become "tired of kissing the dead" ("Morning—A Death"—one of his many puns). He tastes the blood of the dead upon him often in his poems, and he experiments obviously with almost every device known to self-conscious poets: allusion, consonance, assonance, internal and true rhyme (including two dactyls that are excruciatingly memorable), and dramatic monologue. Paquet shares the anguished awareness of Richard Currey, whose *Fatal Light* (Dutton, 1988) also shows how a medical attendant feels.

BRUCE WEIGL'S poems can be read sequentially, from "Sailing to Bien Hoa" to "What Saves Us." Like so many other Vietnam veterans who are also artists, Weigl is compelled to return to what W. D. Ehrhart has called "the single most important experience of [one's] life." Wracked by his experiences in the war, Weigl has to date written more important retrospective poems than has anyone else, and his technical mastery of image (one should watch his use of weather and black clouds) accentuates his apocalyptic vision. "Song of Napalm" shows Weigl's adroit juxtaposition of placid vistas with war scenes, and only the somewhat obscure ending of "What Saves Us" keeps this poem from being as good as McDonald's "The Winter before the War" as a testament to and explanation of what going to war is all about.

A PERSONAL NOTE

My work on this anthology has been hardly a labor of love, but rather a labor of commitment. Those who participated in the Vietnam War know well the phrase "It don't mean nothin"—and I confess to having often wished that I could write off the war with the same phrase.

"It don't mean nothin," however, does not mean that the speaker (who *must* be a Vietnam veteran) does not care. Quite the opposite. This phrase is the universal statement (often unvoiced by the millions of Americans who just did their duty, who are not "traumatized," and who are now moving into positions of extreme responsibility) of men and women who are angry and frustrated at what they see as the bullshit of everyday existence perpetuated by people who have lost touch with what really counts.

"Don't mean nothin" is *the* angry phrase of the Vietnam veteran—and if you ask one if he or she has ever read the poetry written about the war, you'll get a shrug. A few will tell you that Steve Mason is the "Poet Laureate of the Vietnam War." Other vets will tell you that Steve Mason wrote *Chickenhawk* (it was Robert Mason), the best prose narrative about helicopter combat. Something must mean something.

If you submit a questionnaire to college students, as I have often, that asks basic questions about the Vietnam War: when it started, when it ended, who fought, who won—you would gag at the responses. However, the generation that was born during the Vietnam War is beginning to realize that it knows absolutely *nothing* about that war, and to them, their ignorance does mean something. To me, their honest expression of ignorance makes my life worthwhile.

This collection of poetry, albeit only a representative sample (as W. D. Ehrhart mentions in his introduction), shows what the war was to the sensitive, aware, literate people who hung their asses out for their country—a decision that, given alternatives, all thinking men and women must make at some time in their lives. These poems *do* mean something, and I've read many of them to audiences of both veterans (10%) and nonveterans (90%).

What has fascinated me is this: while they're listening, the vets watch the nonvets in the audience, and when the kids (who are about the same age as those who served in Vietnam) cry, so do the vets. So it all does mean something—as Homer, who never lifted a spear, understood.

Such is the power of poetry.

Anyone who ignores this book does so at his or her future peril.

John Clark Pratt
Vietnam, Thailand, Laos—1969-70

CONTENTS

INTRODUCTION

When the opportunity to edit this anthology was offered to me, I jumped at it with about the same enthusiasm one might muster when confronted with the prospect of having to spend a sunny Sunday afternoon cleaning out the cellar. My reluctance was twofold:

First, since 1965, when I first considered enlisting in the U.S. Marine Corps, Vietnam has been a permanent fact of my life, a chronic condition, a shadow companion as welcome as a tattoo with an ex-girlfriend's name on it. Over the course of twenty-three years, it has become less a place or a war than a state of mind. Each time I think I am finally free of it, there it is again. I need to do another book about Vietnam like I need to drive a nail into my head.

Second, to serve as editor for a body of work to which I am also a contributor is, at best, an extremely uncomfortable task. For starters, the inherent conflict of interest regarding my own work is obvious, and even the mere appearance of having been self-serving is distasteful to me. Moreover, it means having to choose—or not choose—other poets who, in many cases, have long since come to be fond acquaintances and even dear friends.

I agreed to edit the book, despite my reservations, because it is an important book, and like so much else involving the poetry of the Vietnam War, it was not likely to be done at all (and certainly no time soon) if I didn't do it myself. That I do not seem to be able to escape the Vietnam War may well be a kind of cosmic payback for my ill-considered eagerness to go to war in the first place. That I keep finding myself in the editor's seat (this is the fourth time in twelve years) is, however, the simple result of the failure of more objective and more scholarly people to acknowledge and deal with the vast body of poetry to which the Vietnam War has given rise.

This vast body of poetry is a phenomenon unparalleled in American literature. No previous American war, with the possible exception of the American Civil War, has produced anything like it (this may be true as well of other forms of literary expression). I could suggest some explanations for this, but these lie beyond the scope of this book. Someday a true scholar, perhaps some diligent young graduate student seeking an untapped theme for a doctoral dissertation, will take the time to give the matter the attention it deserves. My immediate concern is for what was produced, not why.

And in fact, my focus in this book is even more narrow than that. Here I offer only those poets whom I believe to be the most significant voices to have written about the actual experience of Vietnam: the war itself and its impact on those who fought there. Some of them, like Michael Casey, Horace Coleman, and Basil T. Paquet, produced most of their work relatively early on and have published little or nothing since. Some, like D. F. Brown and Yusef Komunyakaa, have begun to emerge only in recent years. The rest have been writing and publishing more or less continuously for up to two decades. Jan Barry holds a special place in Vietnam War poetry, not only for his own pioneering poems dating back to the 1960s, but also for his selfless efforts to publish and promote the poetry of others.

No two of these poets are alike. John Balaban was a conscientious objector during the war, but did his alternative service in Vietnam. Bryan Alec Floyd did not serve in Vietnam at all, though he is a Vietnam-era veteran. Walter McDonald was an Air Force career officer and pilot. Gerald McCarthy was in the Marines; Bruce Weigl, the First Air Mobile Cavalry. Each has his own experience to tell, his own style, his own perspective.

But all of them share several common traits: each is a powerful witness to the war and its aftermath; each has a direct connection to the war itself that emerges as an authentic voice commanding authority, and each is likely to be remembered and read in years to come. Although I am not a scholar, I have been immersed in American poetry about the Vietnam War since 1971. And while I have read a great many superior poems over the years, by veterans and nonveterans alike, the poets I have selected here are the ones that have most moved me, that seem most worthy of historical and literary attention.

Some other person, of course, might well have chosen differently with regard to this poet or that poem. My selections are inevitably subjective. (As far back as undergraduate school, I began to suspect that all such judgements are based ultimately on a kind of gut instinct, a certain feeling that does not lend itself easily to explanation, but now is not the time for that discussion either.) I have chosen as carefully and honestly as I know how. But as one reads these poems, one must be aware that they are only the tip of the proverbial iceberg.

Indeed, I gave serious consideration to including several other poets in this anthology: D. C. Berry, author of *saigon cemetery* (University of Georgia Press, 1972); Frank A. Cross, Jr., author of *Reminders* (Seven Buffaloes Press, 1986); David Huddle, whose twelve-poem cycle "Tour of Duty" appeared in *Vietnam Flashbacks* (Pig Iron Press, 1984); and Larry Rottmann, whose poems can be found in *Winning Hearts and Minds: War Poems by Vietnam Veterans* (1st Casualty Press/McGraw Hill, 1972). That none of them is represented here may reflect more on me than on them.

The same might be said for Dick Shea (*Vietnam Simply*, Pro Tem Publishers, 1967), Earl E. Martin (*A Poet Goes to War*, Big Sky Books, 1970), MacAvoy Layne (*How Audie Murphy Died in Vietnam*, Anchor Books, 1973), Perry Oldham (*Vinh Long*, Northwoods Press, 1976), Robert Schlosser (*The Humidity Readings*, Samisdat Associates, 1981), Doug Rawlings (*Survivor's Manual*, Samisdat Associates, 1982), R. L. Barth (*Forced-Marching to the Styx*, Perivale Press, 1983), or Steve Mason (*Johnny's Song*, Bantam Books, 1985). I have also admired individual poems that I've read or heard by Patrick Worth Gray, Norma J. Griffiths, Lamont Steptoe, and others.

Most of these poets, and many more whom I have not taken the time to name, can be found in one or more of the following anthologies: the previously mentioned *Winning Hearts and Minds*, edited by Jan Barry, Basil T. Paquet and Larry Rottmann; *Listen: The War*, Tony Dater and Fred Kiley, eds., United States Air Force Academy Association of Graduates, 1973; *Demilitarized Zones: Veterans After Vietnam*, Jan Barry and W. D. Ehrhart, eds., East River Anthology, 1976; *Peace Is Our Profession*, Jan Barry, ed., East River Anthology, 1981; the previously mentioned *Vietnam Flashbacks*, edited by Jim Villani and Rose Sayre; *Tour of Duty*, Cranston Sedrick Knight, ed., Samisdat Associates, 1986; and my own *Carrying the Darkness: the Poetry of the Vietnam War*, published in 1985 and reissued by Texas Tech University Press in 1989.

Other anthologies, those reflecting primarily the reactions of nonveterans to the war in Vietnam, include *A Poetry Reading Against the Vietnam War*, Robert Bly and David Ray, eds., The Sixties Press, 1966; *Where Is Vietnam?*, Walter Lowenfels, ed., Anchor Books, 1967; *Out of the Shadow of War*, Denise Levertov, ed., War Resisters League 1968 Peace Calendar; and *Poetry Against the War*, a special issue of *Poetry* published in September, 1972.

All of these poets and anthologies offer, of necessity, strictly American perspectives (as does the current collection). Although many of these books are long since out of print and hard to come by, the Vietnamese point of view (or, more accurately, points of view) is even more elusive. Works by Vietnamese poets written in or translated into English that I know of include Thich Nhat Hanh's *Viet Nam Poems* (1967) and *The Cry of Vietnam* (1968), both from Unicorn Press; *Of Quiet Courage*, Jacqui Chagnon and Don Luce, eds., Indochina Mobile Education Project, 1974; John Balaban's *Ca Dao Vietnam*, Unicorn Press, 1980; *Flowers from Hell*, Huynh Sanh Thong, ed., Southeast Asia Studies, Yale University, 1984; *Shallow Graves*, Wendy Larson and Tran Thi Nga, Random House, 1986; and various editions of Ho Chi Minh's *Prison Diary* (the one I have was published by Red River Press in 1983. I have not come upon any poetry dealing with the French experience in Indochina and available in English, though it may well exist, nor have I encountered poetry by Australians, New Zealanders, Koreans, Thais or Filipinos, all of whom fought in Vietnam—not to mention Laotians or Cambodians, whose countries were also devastated by the war.).

Undoubtedly, this brief survey is not comprehensive, but it ought at least to reinforce the point I made earlier about the current anthology representing only the tip of the iceberg. Still, even though the body of Vietnam War poetry is enormous, the twelve poets included here have not ended up in this book merely by chance, the vagaries of human subjectivity not withstanding. Each has a legitimate claim to inclusion. They represent, for me, the terrible beauty that Vietnam engendered in sensitive hearts, the curious grace with which the human spirit can endow even the ugliest of realities—and Vietnam was surely as ugly a reality as I ever want to encounter. Each of these poets has become something more than a "Vietnam poet;" each has contributed materially to the body and soul of American literature.

Aside from a few passing remarks that one might construe as editorial comments, I have refrained from saying anything about the war itself. This book is neither history nor political commentary. The events of the war can be found in any number of chronologies, and how those events ought to be interpreted will be argued by historians and politicians, generals and academics for generations to come—with no one likely to be the wiser for it. But if one wants to know the essence of the Vietnam War, how it felt and smelled and tasted, what it did to those who fought it and why it will not go away, I believe one is likely to find more truth in these poems than in any history ever written. There is much to be learned from poetry, and these poets are able teachers.

Whether I belong among them is a decision I would rather someone else had made. In the absence of that, I have chosen to include myself; I am tempted to make a case for that decision, but that would only compound my discomfort. The poems will have to speak for themselves, and I will have to live with it. I could not, however, bring myself to choose which poems of mine to include, or how many. I am grateful to Judith Keeling, editor, Texas Tech University Press, for taking at least that much of the burden from me.

Lastly, I wish to thank my wife, Anne, for her patience and support and love, for believing in me more than I believe in myself. And I would like to apologize to my daughter, Leela, for my spending so much time with this book at her expense. My apology won't mean much to her now, but perhaps someday when she is old enough to read, and old enough to begin to imagine what war is and what it costs, she may finally understand why daddy was always so busy that long ago summer of 1988.

W. D. Ehrhart
Philadelphia
July 1988

JOHN BALABAN

John Balaban was born in 1943 in Philadelphia, Pennsylvania. A conscientious objector, he did alternative service in Vietnam, 1967-69, with International Voluntary Services and the Committee of Responsibility to Save War-Injured Children. Subsequently, he returned to Vietnam, 1971-72, to collect the oral folk poetry of farmers and fishermen. He holds a B.A. from Pennsylvania State University and an A.M. from Harvard. He is a winner of the Lamont Award from the Academy of American Poets, a National Book Award nominee, and the recipient of two fellowships each from the National Endowment for the Arts and the National Endowment for the Humanities, as well as three Fulbright Fellowships. He is currently professor of English at Pennsylvania State University.

Balaban's work has appeared in *TriQuarterly, Ploughshares, The Nation, Sewanee Review, Southern Review, American Scholar, Chelsea, Prairie Schooner, New Letters,* and the *New York Times.* He is author of the text for Geoffrey Clifford's photographic study *Vietnam: The Land We Never Knew* (New York: Chronicle Books, 1989). In addition, Balaban has published the following volumes:

POETRY
Vietnam Poems. Oxford, England: Carcanet Press, 1970.
After Our War. Pittsburgh, Pa.: University of Pittsburgh Press, 1974.
Scrisori de Peste Mare [*Letters from Across the Sea*]. Cluj, Romania: Dacia Press, 1979.
Blue Mountain. Greensboro, N.C.: Unicorn Press, 1982.

FICTION
Coming Down Again. San Diego: Harcourt, Brace, Jovanovich, 1985; New York: Fireside Books, 1989.
The Hawk's Tale. San Diego: Harcourt, Brace, Jovanovich, 1988. (For children.)

TRANSLATIONS
Vietnamese Folk Poetry. Greensboro, N.C.: Unicorn Press, 1974.
Ca Dao Vietnam: A Bilingual Anthology of Vietnamese Folk Poetry. Greensboro, N.C.: Unicorn Press, 1980.

The Guard at the Binh Thuy Bridge

How still he stands as mists begin to move,
as morning, curling, billows creep across
his cooplike, concrete sentry perched mid bridge
over mid-muddy river. Stares at bush-green banks
which bristle rifles, mortars, men—perhaps.
No convoys shake the timbers. No sound
but water slapping boatsides, banksides, pilings.
He's slung his carbine barrel down to keep
the boring dry, and two banana-clips instead of one
are taped to make, now, forty rounds instead

7

of twenty. Droplets bead from stock to sight;
they bulb, then strike his boot. He scrapes his heel,
and sees no boxbombs floating towards his bridge.
Anchored in red morning mist a narrow junk
rocks its weight. A woman kneels on deck
staring at lapping water. Wets her face.
Idly the thick Rach Binh Thuy slides by.
He aims. At her. Then drops his aim. Idly.

Along the Mekong

1. Crossing on the Mekong Ferry,
Reading the August 14 *New Yorker*

Near mud-tide mangrove swamps, under the drilling sun
the glossy cover, styled green print, struck the eye:
trumpet-burst yellow blossoms, grapevine leaves,
—nasturtiums or pumpkin flowers? They twined
in tangles by our cottage in Pennsylvania.
Inside, another article by Thomas Whiteside.
2, 4, 5-T, teratogenicity in births;
South Vietnam 1/7th defoliated; residue
in rivers, foods, and mother's milk.
With a scientific turn of mind I can understand
that malformations in lab mice may not occur in children
but when, last week, I ushered hare-lipped, tusk-toothed kids
to surgery in Saigon, I wondered, what did they drink
that I have drunk. What dioxin, picloram, arsenic
have knitted in my cells, in my wife now carrying
our first child. Pigs were squealing in a truck.
Through the slats, I saw one lather the foam in his mouth.

2. River Market

Under the tattered umbrellas, piles of live eels
sliding in flat tin pans. Catfish flip for air.
Sunfish, gutted and gilled, cheek plates snipped.
Baskets of ginger roots, ginseng, and garlic cloves;
pails of shallots, chives, green citrons. Rice grain
in pyramids. Pig halves knotted with mushy fat.
Beef haunches hung from fist-size hooks. Sorcerers,

8

palmists, and, under a tarp: thick incense, candles.
Why, a reporter, or a cook, could write this poem
if he had learned dictation. But what if I said,
simply suggested, that all this blood fleck,
muscle rot, earth root and earth leaf, scraps
of glittery scales, fine white grains, fast talk,
gut grime, crab claws, bright light, sweetest smells
—Said: a human self; a mirror held up before.

3. Waiting for a Boat to Cross Back

Slouched on a bench under some shade,
I overhear that two men shot each other on the street,
and I watch turkey cocks drag cornstalk fans
like mad, rivaling kings in Kabuki
sweeping huge sleeve and brocaded train.
The drab hens huddle, beak to beak,
in queenly boredom of rhetoric and murder.
A mottled cur with a grease-paint grin
laps up fish scales and red, saw-toothed gills
gutted from panfish at the river's edge.

Mau Than

A Poem at Tet for To Lai Chanh

1

Friend, the Old Man that was last year
has had his teeth kicked in; in tears
he spat back blood and bone, and died.
Pielike, the moon has carved the skies
a year's worth to the eve. It is Tet
as I sit musing at your doorstep,
as the yellowed leaves scratch and clutter.
The garden you dug and plotted
before they drafted you, is now
stony, dry, and wanting a trowel.
"For my wife," you said, taking a plum,
but the day never came nor will it come
to bring your bride from Saigon.
Still the boats fetch stone, painted eyes on

their prows, plowing the banana-green river;
and neighbor children splash and shiver
where junks wait to unload their rock.
But shutters locked, the door of your house is locked.

2

A year it was of barbarities
each heaped on the other like stones
on a man stoned to death.
One counts the ears on the GI's belt.
Market meats come wrapped in wrappers
displaying Viet Cong disemboweled.
Cries come scattering like shot.
You heard them and I heard them.
The blessed unmaimed may have too.
So many go stumping about.
The night you left I turned off Hoa Binh
and saw a mined jeep, the charred family.
A Vietnamese cop minded the wreckage;
his gold buck teeth were shining
in a smile like a bright brass whistle.
Can you tell me how the Americans,
officers and men, on the night of
the mortaring, in the retching hospital,
could snap flash-photos of the girl whose
vagina was gouged out by mortar fragments?
One day we followed in a cortege
of mourners, among the mourners, slowly walking,
hearing the clop of the monk's knocking stick.

3

If there were peace, this river would be
a peaceful place. Here at your door
thoughts arrive like rainwater, dotting,
overspreading a dry, porous rock.
In a feathery drizzle, a man and wife
are fishing the river. The sidling waves
slap at her oar as she ladles the water
and fixes the boat with bored precision.
His taut wrists fling whirring weights;
the flying net swallows a circle of fish.
His ear wears a raindrop like a jewel.

Here at evening one might be as quiet
as the rain blowing faintly off
the eaves of a rice boat sliding home.
Coming to this evening
after a rain, I found a buff bird
perched in the silvery-green branches
of a water-shedding spruce. It was
perched like a peaceful thought. Then
I thought of the Book of Luke and, indeed,
of the nobleman who began a sojourn
to find a kingdom and return.

4

Out of the night, wounded
with the gibberings of dogs,
wheezing with the squeaks of rats,
out of the night, its belly split
by jet whine and mortar blast,
scissored by the claws of children,
street-sleepers, ripping their way free
from cocoons of mosquito netting
to flee the rupturing bursts
and the air dancing with razors
—out, I came, to safe haven.
Nor looked, nor asked further.
Who would? What more? I said.
I said: Feed and bathe me.
In Japan I climbed Mt. Hiei in midwinter.
The deer snuffled my mittens.
The monkeys came to beg.
I met Moses meeting God in the clouds.
The cold wind cleared my soul.
The mountain was hidden in mist. Friend,
I am back to gather the blood in a cup.

Opening Le Ba Khon's Dictionary

So the Soul, that Drop, that Ray
of the clear Fountain of Eternal Day,
Could it within the humane Power be seen.
—ANDREW MARVELL, "On A Drop of Dew"

The ink-specked sheets feel like cigar leaf;
its crackling spine flutters up a mildewed must.
Unlike the lacquered box which dry-warp detonated
—shattering pearled poet, moon, and willow pond—
the book survived, but begs us both go back
to the Bibliothèque in the Musée at the Jardin in Saigon,
where I would lean from ledges of high windows
to see the zoo's pond, isled with Chinese pavilion,
arched bridge where kids fed popcorn to gulping carp,
and shaded benches, where whores fanned their make-up,
at ease because a man who feeds the peacocks
can't be that much of a beast. A boatride,
a soda, a stroll through the flower beds.
On weekends the crowds could forget the war.
At night police tortured men in the bear pits,
one night a man held out the bag of his own guts,
which streamed and weighed in his open hands,
and offered them to a bear. Nearby, that night
the moon was caught in willows by the pond,
shone scattered in droplets on the flat lotus pads,
each bead bright like the dew in Marvell's rose.

The Dragonfish

Brown men shock the brown pools with nets.
fishing for mudfish, carp and *ca loc*,
they step and stalk the banks; hurl;
stand, then squat heronlike in the
shadow-stretching, red evening dusk.

The pond is lovely where they fish,
one of many in a marshy field
linking delta paddies about Cao Lanh.
Phenol streaks, chartreuse and smoke blue,

curl, clot and twirl over the manila-bright,
sun-slanting surface, while silver chubs
flash after garbage scraps chugging out,
churning up, from an opening drain.

Five old tombs shadow the pond's far edge.
Their dripping stones are cut in characters
which no one, now, can read. Ghosts
of landlords click their tallies there.
Rain roils the water. Ducks dally
through twining blue morning-glory
trellising in spirals
over concertina barbed wire.
Like swallows or a weaver's shuttles,
darting jets, F-105s,
ply the curling fringes of the storm.

Rain spatters—wind scatters—
the water turned gun-barrel blue.
In sheeting rain, a wet dog grins
from a worn tomb's washing steps.
The dog snuffles a hen's feather.
It crackles old bones.

Far out in deserted paddies
more cratered than the moon,
guerrillas of the Front hide themselves
beneath slabs of rain-eaten tombs:
patient as lampwicks.

In squalling waters, North and South,
fishermen dredge, draw, dragnet up
a heavy fish, a dragon fish,
a land in the shape of the dragonfish.

After Our War

After our war, the dismembered bits
—all those pierced eyes, ear slivers, jaw splinters,
gouged lips, odd tibias, skin flaps, and toes—
came squinting, wobbling, jabbering back.

The genitals, of course, were the most bizarre,
inching along roads like glowworms and slugs.
The living wanted them back, but good as new.
The dead, of course, had no use for them.
And the ghosts, the tens of thousands of abandoned souls
who had appeared like swamp fog in the city streets,
on the evening altars, and on doorsills of cratered homes,
also had no use for the scraps and bits
because, in their opinion, they looked good without them.
Since all things naturally return to their source,
these snags and tatters arrived, with immigrant uncertainty,
in the United States. It was almost home.
So, now, one can sometimes see a friend or a famous man talking
with an extra pair of lips glued and yammering on his cheek,
and this is why handshakes are often unpleasant,
why it is better, sometimes, not to look another in the eye,
why, at your daughter's breast thickens a hard keloidal scar.
After the war, with such Cheshire cats grinning in our trees,
will the ancient tales still tell us new truths?
Will the myriad world surrender new metaphor?
After our war, how will love speak?

For Mrs. Cam, Whose Name Means "Printed Silk"

The ancients liked to write of natural beauty.
—Ho Chi Minh, "On Reading *The Ten Thousand Poets*"

In Vietnam, poets brushed on printed silk
those poems about clouds, mountains, and love.
But now their poems are cased in steel.

You lived beyond the Pass of Clouds
along the Perfume River, in Hué,
whose name means "lily."

The war has blown away your past.
No poem can call it back.
How does one start over?

You raise your kids in southern California;
run a key punch from 9:00 to 5:00,
and walk the beach each evening,

marveling at curls broken bare in crushed shells,
at the sheen and cracks of laved, salted wood,
at the pearling blues of rock-stuck mussels

all broken, all beautiful, accidents
which remind you of your life, lost friends
and pieces of poems which made you whole.

In tidal pools, the pipers wade
on twiggy legs, stabbing for starfish
with scissoring, poking, needle bills.

The wide Pacific flares in sunset.
Somewhere over there was once your home.
You study the things which start from scratch.

Nicely like a pearl is a poem
begun with an accidental speck
from the ocean of the actual.

A grain, a grit, which once admitted
irritates the mantle of thought
and coats itself in lacquers of the mind.

April 30, 1975

for Bui Ngoc Huong

The evening Nixon called his last troops off,
the church bells tolled across our states.
We leaned on farmhouse porch pilings, our eyes
wandering the lightning bug meadow thick with mist,
and counted tinny peals clanking out
through oaks around the church belltower.
You asked, "Is it peace, or only a bell ringing?"

This night the war has finally ended.
My wife and I sit on a littered park bench
sorting out our shared and separate lives
in the dark, in silence, before a quiet pond
where ducks tug slimy papers and bits of soggy bread.
City lights have reddened the bellies of fumed clouds
like trip flares scorching skies over a city at war.

In whooshing traffic at the park's lit edge,
red brake lights streak to sudden halts:
a ski-masked man staggers through lanes,
maced by a girl he tried to mug.
As he crashes to curb under mercury lamps,
a man snakes towards him, wetting his lips,
twirling the root of his tongue like a dial.

Some kids have burnt a bum on Brooklyn Bridge.
Screaming out of sleep, he flares the causeway.
The war returns like figures in a dream.
In Vietnam, pagodas chime their bells.
"A Clear Mind spreads like the wind.
By the Lo waterfalls, free and high,
you wash away the dust of life."

In Celebration of Spring

Our Asian war is over; others have begun.
Our elders, who tried to mortgage lies,
are disgraced, or dead, and already
the brokers are picking their pockets
for the keys and the credit cards.

In delta swamp in a united Vietnam,
a Marine with a bullfrog for a face,
rots in equatorial heat. An eel
slides through the cage of his bared ribs.
At night, on the old battlefields, ghosts,
like patches of fog, lurk into villages

to maunder on doorsills of cratered homes,
while all across the U.S.A.
the wounded walk about and wonder where to go.

And today, in the simmer of lyric sunlight,
the chrysalis pulses in its mushy cocoon,
under the bark on a gnarled root of an elm.
In the brilliant creek, a minnow flashes
delirious with gnats. The turtle's heart
quickens its taps in the warm bank sludge.
As she chases a frisbee spinning in sunlight,
a girl's breasts bounce full and strong;
a boy's stomach, as he turns, is flat and strong.

Swear by the locust, by dragonflies on ferns,
by the minnow's flash, the tremble of a breast,
by the new earth spongy under our feet:
that as we grow old, we will not grow evil,
that although our garden seeps with sewage,
and our elders think it's up for auction—swear
by this dazzle that does not wish to leave us—
that we will be keepers of a garden, nonetheless.

News Update

*for Erhart, Gitelson, Flynn and Stone,
happily dead and gone.*

Well, here I am in the *Centre Daily Times*
back to back with the page one refugees
fleeing the crossfire, pirates, starvation.
Familiar faces. We followed them
through defoliated forests, cratered fields,
past the blasted water buffalo,
the shredded tree lines, the human head
dropped on the dusty road, eyes open,
the dusty road which called you all to death.

One skims the memory like a moviola
editing out the candid shots: Sean Flynn
dropping his camera and grabbing a gun

to muster the charge and retake the hill.
"That boy," the black corporal said,
"do in real life what his daddy do in movies."
Dana Stone, in an odd moment of mercy,
sneaking off from Green Beret assassins
to the boy they left for dead in the jungle.
Afraid of the pistol's report, Stone shut his eyes
and collapsed the kid's throat with a bayonet.
Or, Erhart, sitting on his motorcycle
smiling and stoned in the Free Strike Zone
as he filmed the ammo explosion at Lai Khe.
It wasn't just a macho game. Marie-Laure de Decker
photographed the man aflame on the public lawn.
She wept and shook and cranked her Pentax
until a cop smashed it to the street. Then
there was the girl returned from captivity
with a steel comb fashioned from a melted-down tank,
or some such cliché, and engraved: "To Sandra
From the People's Fifth Battalion, Best Wishes."

Christ, most of them are long dead. Tim Page
wobbles around with a steel plate in his head.
Gitelson roamed the Delta in cut-away blue jeans
like a hippy Johnny Appleseed with a burlap sack
full of seeds and mimeographed tips for farmers
until we pulled him from the canal. His brains
leaked on my hands and knee. Or me, yours truly,
agape in the Burn Ward in Da Nang, a quonset hut,
a half a garbage can that smelled like Burger King,
listening to whimpers and nitrate fizzing on flesh
in a silence that simmered like a fly in a wound.

And here I am, ten years later,
written up in the local small town press
for popping a loud-mouth punk in the choppers.
Oh, big sighs. Windy sighs. And ghostly laughter.

Thoughts before Dawn

for Mary Bui Thi Khuy, 1944-1969

The bare oaks rock and snowcrust tumbles down.
The creaking eave woke me, thinking of you
crushed by a truck thirteen years ago
when the drunk ARVN lost the wheel.

We brought to better care the nearly lost,
the boy burned by white phosphorus, chin
glued to his chest; the scalped girl;
the triple amputee from the road-mined bus;
the kid without a jaw; the one with no nose.
You never wept in front of them, but waited
until the gurney rolled them into surgery.
I guess that's what amazed me most.
Why didn't you fall apart or quit?

Once, we flew two patched kids home,
getting in by Army chopper,
a Huey Black Cat that skimmed the sea.
When the gunner opened up on a whale
you closed your eyes and covered your ears
and your small body shook in your silk *ao dai*.
Oh, Mary. In this arctic night, awake in my bed
I rehearse your smile, bright white teeth,
the funny way you rode your Honda 50, perched
so straight, silky hair bunned up in a brim hat,
front brim blown back, and dark glasses.
Brave woman, I hope you never saw the truck.

Story

The guy picked me up north of Santa Fe
where the red hills, dotted with piñon,
loop down from the Divide into mesas and plain.
I was standing out there—just me, my pack,
and the gila monsters—when he hauled his Buick
off the road in a sputter of cinders and dust.
And got out, a gray-bearded, 6-foot, 300-pounder,

who stretched and said, "Do you want to drive?"
So I drove and he told me the story of his life.
How his father was a Russian Jew who got zapped
by the Mob during Prohibition, how he quit school
at fifteen and got a job as a DJ in Detroit,
how he sold flatware on the road and made a mint,
how he respected his wife, but didn't love her,
how he hit it big in radio and tv, how he fell in love,
how he found himself, at 50, in intensive care
where his wife, his kids, his girlfriend, and his rabbi
huddled in silence about his bed when his doctor
came in and whispered that maybe he ought to ask
the wife and the girlfriend to alternate visits
'because it wasn't too good for his heart.'
"What about your kids?" I asked. "What do they do?"
"My daughter runs our store. My son is dead."
He studied a distant peak and didn't continue.
"What did he die of?"—"He died of suicide.
. . . No, that's not right. Nixon killed him.
My son was a sweet kid, hated guns and violence
and then, during that fucking war, he hijacked a plane
and flew it to Cuba. He shot himself in Havana."
He studied the peak, then grinned and said,
"Brave little fucker, wasn't he?" I nodded.

That night, camping in a patch of mesquite and pine,
as I rocked a log to roll it towards my fire,
I saw a mouse squashed in its nest of willow down.
Its brave heart thumped as I held it in my hand
where it skittered to escape just before it died.
I laid it down by the glow of the campfire
which flickered like a lamp in the circling trees.
In the distance, the highway whined like gnats,
and, in the east, a full moon was on the rise.

Mr. Giai's Poem

The French ships shelled Haiphong then took the port.
Mr. Giai was running down a road, mobilized,
with two friends, looking for their unit in towns
where thatch and geese lay shattered on the roads

and smoke looped up from cratered yards. A swarm
of bullock carts and bicycles streamed against them
as trousered women strained with children, chickens,
charcoal and rice towards Hanoi in the barrage lull.
Then, Giai said, they saw just stragglers.
Ahead, the horizon thumped with bombs.

At an empty inn they tried their luck
though the waiter said he'd nothing left.
"Just a coffee," said Mr. Giai. "A sip
of whisky," said one friend. "A cigarette," the other.
Miraculously, these each appeared. Serene,
they sat a while, then went to fight.
Giai wrote a poem about that pause for *Ve Quoc Quan*,
the Army paper. Critics found the piece bourgeois.

Forty years of combat now behind him
—Japanese, Americans, and French.
Wounded twice, deployed in jungles for nine years,
his son just killed in Kampuchea,
Giai tells this tale to three Americans
each young enough to be his son:
an ex-Marine once rocketed in Hué,
an Army grunt, mortared at Bong Son,
a C.O. hit by a stray of shrapnel,

all four now silent in the floating restaurant
rocking on moorlines in the Saigon river.
Crabshells and beer bottles litter their table.
A rat runs a rafter overhead. A wave slaps by.
"That moment," Giai adds, "was a little like now."
They raise their glasses to the river's amber light,
all four as quiet as if carved in ivory.

Words for My Daughter

About eight of us were nailing up forts
in the mulberry grove behind Reds' house
when his mother started screeching and
all of us froze except Reds—fourteen, huge
as a hippo—who sprang out of the tree so fast

the branch nearly bobbed me off. So fast,
he hit the ground running, hammer in hand,
and seconds after he got in the house
we heard thumps like someone beating a tire
off a rim   his dad's howls the screen door
banging open   Saw   Reds barreling out
through the tall weeds towards the highway
the father stumbling after his fat son
who never looked back across the thick swale
of teazel and black-eyed susans until it was safe
to yell fuck you at the skinny drunk
stamping around barefoot and holding his ribs.

Another time, the Connelly kid came home to find
his alcoholic mother getting fucked by the milkman.
Bobby broke a milkbottle and jabbed the guy
humping on his mom. I think it really happened
because none of us would loosely mention that
wraith of a woman who slippered around her house
and never talked to anyone, not even her kids.
Once a girl ran past my porch
with a dart in her back, her open mouth
pumping like a guppy's, her eyes wild.
Later that summer, or maybe the next,
the kids hung her brother from an oak.
Before they hoisted him, yowling and heavy
on the clothesline, they made him claw the creekbank
and eat worms. I don't know why his neck didn't snap.

Reds had another nickname you couldn't say
or he'd beat you up: "Honeybun."
His dad called him that when Reds was little.

*

So, these were my playmates. I love them still
for their justice and valor and desperate loves
twisted in shapes of hammer and shard.
I want you to know about their pain
and about the pain they could loose on others.
If you're reading this, I hope you will think,

Well, my Dad had it rough as a kid, so what?
If you're reading this, you can read the news
and you know that children suffer worse.

                          *

Worse for me is a cloud of memories
still drifting off the South China Sea,
like the 9-year old boy, naked and lacerated,
thrashing in his pee on a steel operating table
and yelling "Dau. Dau," while I, trying to translate
in the mayhem of Tet for surgeons who didn't know
who this boy was or what happened to him, kept asking
"Where? Where's the pain?" until a surgeon
said "Forget it. His ears are blown."

                          *

I remember your first Hallow'een
when I held you on my chest and rocked you,
so small your toes didn't touch my lap
as I smelled your fragrant peony head
and cried because I was so happy and because
I heard, in no metaphorical way, the awful chorus
of Soeur Anicet's orphans writhing in their cribs.
Then the doorbell rang and a tiny Green Beret
was saying trick-or-treat and I thought *oh oh*
but remembered it was Hallow'een and where I was.
I smiled at the evil midget, his map-light and night
paint, his toy knife for slitting throats, said,
"How ya doin', soldier?" and, still holding you asleep
in my arms, gave him a Mars Bar. To his father
waiting outside in fatigues I hissed, "You, shit,"
and saw us, child, in a pose I know too well.

I want you to know the worst and be free from it.
I want you to know the worst and still find good.
Day by day, as you play nearby or laugh
with the ladies at Peoples Bank as we go around town
and I find myself beaming like a fool,
I suspect I am here less for your protection
than you are here for mine, as if you were sent
to call me back into our helpless tribe.

Notes

"Mau Than" In the midst of the Lunar New Year celebrations in 1968 (*mau than*— the Year of the Monkey), the Viet Cong and North Vietnamese launched throughout South Vietnam a major series of attacks that came to be known as the Tet Offensive.

There are two biblical references in the poem—one to the New Testament Gospel According to St. Luke, Chapter 19; the other to the Old Testament book of Exodus, also Chapter 19.

"Opening Le Ba Khon's Dictionary" Le Ba Khon was the author of a Vietnamese dictionary.

Bibliothèque in the Musée at the Jardin—the museum library of the Saigon Botanical Gardens; the botanical gardens also had a small zoo, including bears which were kept in the bear pits referred to later in the poem.

"After Our War" The Cheshire Cat is a character in Lewis Carroll's *Alice in Wonderland.*

"April 30, 1975" The date in the title refers to the actual end of the Vietnam war, the day Viet Cong and North Vietnamese troops occupied Saigon.

The reference in the first line is to President Richard Nixon's signing of the Paris Peace Accords in January 1973, which brought an end to direct involvement in the war by U.S. troops. It was celebrated at the time as "the end of the war," but brought neither an end to the fighting nor an end to the United States' involvement in the war.

The last three lines are taken from a Vietnamese folk poem.

"News Update" Marie-Laure de Decker was a journalist who witnessed and attempted to photograph the self-immolation of a Buddhist monk in Saigon in 1971. Such self-immolations in protest of the war occurred all too frequently in the early and mid-1960s, but became less frequent after the Saigon government cracked down on internal dissent in the later stages of the war.

Johnny Appleseed is the popular name of John Chapman, a legendary figure of early nineteenth-century America, who supposedly traveled through the West planting apple orchards.

"Mr. Giai's Poem" The first two stanzas of the poem refer to the French naval shelling of Haiphong in November 1946, which is generally considered to mark the beginning of the French Indochina War or First Indochina War (1946-1954).

The three Americans in the third stanza are W. D. Ehrhart, Bruce Weigl, and John Balaban, who returned to Vietnam in December 1985.

"Words for My Daughter" Soeur Anicet was a Catholic nun who ran an orphanage in Vietnam.

JAN BARRY

Jan Barry was born in 1943 in Ithaca, New York. He served in the United States Army, 1962-65, as a radio specialist, including service in Vietnam with the Eighteenth Aviation Company, 1962-63. In 1964, he resigned an appointment as a cadet at the United States Military Academy. He was a co-founder of Vietnam Veterans Against the War in 1967. He is currently a journalist and freelance writer. He is also founder and executive director of the Essex County (New Jersey) Office on Peace.

Barry's work has appeared in the *Chicago Sun-Times*, the *Chicago Tribune*, *Freedomways*, the *New York Times*, *Shantih*, *Stone Country*, the *Washington Star*, *Waterways*, *WIN*, and *Young Lawyer*. He has been anthologized in *A People and a Nation: A History of the United States*, *Tour of Duty*, *Vietnam Anthology*, *The Lessons of the Vietnam War*, and *Unwinding the Vietnam War*. Barry has seven published books:

POETRY

Veterans Day. Richford, Vt.: Samisdat, 1982.
War Baby. Richford, Vt.: Samisdat, 1983.
Morning in Moscow. Montclair, N.J.: Candle Press, 1987.
Cold War Blues. Montclair, N.J.: Candle Press, 1988.

EDITED WORKS

With Basil T. Paquet and Larry Rottmann. *Winning Hearts and Minds: War Poems by Vietnam Veterans*. Brooklyn, N.Y.: 1st Casualty Press, 1972; New York: McGraw-Hill, 1972.
With W. D. Ehrhart. *Demilitarized Zones: Veterans After Vietnam*: Perkasie, Pa.: East River Anthology, 1976.
Peace Is Our Profession. Montclair, N.J.: East River Anthology, 1981.

In the Footsteps of Genghis Khan

There, where a French legionnaire
once walked patrol
around the flightline perimeter of the airfield
at Nha Trang,
ten years later I walked,
an American expeditionary forces
soldier on night guard duty
at Nha Trang,
occupied even earlier,
twenty years before
(a year more than my nineteen),
by the Japanese.

Unhaunted by the ghosts, living and dead,
among us
in the red tile-roofed French barracks

or listening in on the old Japanese telephone line
to Saigon,
we went about our military duties,
setting up special forces headquarters
where once a French Foreign Legion post had been,
oblivious to the irony
of Americans walking in the footsteps
of Genghis Khan.

Unencumbered by history,
our own or that of 13th-century Mongol armies
long since fled or buried
by the Vietnamese,
in Nha Trang, in 1962, we just did our jobs:
replacing kepis with berets, "Ah so!" with "Gawd!
Damn!"

Nights in Nha Trang

The girls,
the girls of
Nha Trang
ply their trade
every night   "Monique,
along the beach   Monique come
                               ti ti
                               Monique
                               come you
The peanut   ti ti"
girls,
twelve
and thirteen   "You buy
singing   mango,
                               you buy me?
                               You buy
                               mango,
                               you buy
All   me?"
selling the
fruit

of Nha
Trang
every night
along the
dark
crescent   "You buy
beach   Saigon tea,
                             you buy
                             me?
                             You buy me
                             one
                             Saigon tea?"

A Nun in Ninh Hoa

It was quite a sight for a boy from Tennessee:
a Buddhist nun dressed in fire
sitting proudly amid a solemn, silent crowd,
flames and a smoke plume her terrible costume.

Riding shotgun on a fuel truck convoy,
"just along for the ride,"
Jimmy Sharpe saw a sight this morning
beyond any experience he can describe.

She sat smiling as though mocking the flames.
Her hands, held together in prayer,
slowly parted. Suddenly, she drooped,
sat up, then wilted in the fire.

Safe back at the base, Jimmy's chatter
circled the nightmare he still could taste.
He grinned—shivered—then softly swore:
"Jeesus! How'd we get in this crazy place?"

Floating Petals

See: here, the bougainvillea;
there, the cactus and palm—
 here: the lotus flower:
 there, the bomb-shattered bamboo

of viet-nam

severed flowers, sharded fronds:
 floating in shrapnel,
 sealed in napalm.

Green Hell, Green Death

Green hell of the jungle:
 green fire, green death,
 green ghosts,
 green,
grim bodies

Green jungle all around: hot,
 full of death,
 fox-fire,
 floating ghosts,
ghosts of the quick and the dead   .

Green hell: green bodies:
 the living, from pallor and dirt
 the dying, from gasping breath
 the dead, from blood-drained
wounds: all in green uniforms

Other green bodies: hidden in
 the green jungle
 in green camouflage
 and green branches and twigs:
green leaves covering quick, green limbs

Green hell: green jungle: green bodies:
    green leaves stalking
    green uniforms hunting
    green limbs
in the growth of the ghost jungle

Green ghosts: flitting through green
    trees—
    green fire: from green fingers
    on green guns—
green jungle: green hellfire: green death

Harvest Moon

Pumpkins' crooked grins
on Halloween window ledges
hide candle flames of bamboo villages . . .

glowing behind the orange
decapitated skulls of Asians
staring at shouting masked children
dressed as little spirits of pirates . . .

waving drooping bags of loot
in wild night chases
with soldiers pilgrims witches
skeletons cowboys and revived "Indians."

Here where our farms and towns,
factories and cities and highways lie,
the civilizations that we buried
rise with the harvest moon.

On a city sidewalk gangs of stick-armed
tricksters steal candy from younger ones,
across a quiet village street
a spinster's favorite privy spills,

while down the road
small shapes scatter from a farm
as a field of hay goes up in flames.

Lessons

"What's a patriot, Dad?
Hey, Dad! 'Earth to Dad—
Earth to Dad!'
Get your nose out of
your newspaper!
Help me with my homework!
What's a patriot, Dad?"

"Well, I guess, a person
who loves the land.
Although some people act as if
a patriot's a man
who hates another land."

"Hey, Dad! Don't
give me a lecture—
all I need's
a word! Just a word!
What's a veteran, Dad?
Hey, Dad! DAD!"

"A veteran's what your
father is—" his mother
chimed in, clear across the room.

"Oh, I got it:
somebody who's always out .
of work, home with us
kids—huh, Dad?
Is that what a veteran is?"

"Yep—" Dad got out,
remembering suddenly
the time his youngest son
had stopped breathing
right here at the kitchen table
(with this oldest son screaming,
"Nicky's dead! Nicky's dead!")
and the frantic fight

to find a sign of life,
while dialing the emergency number
for an ambulance.

"What's war? Dad!
You know, Dad! War—war!
Dad! What the hell's war?"

And old Dad blurted out,
still thinking of the desperate
battle one desperate night
to save the baby's life:
"Ten minutes of terror,
after twenty years of anticipation,
and then twenty years of worrying
'when's it going to happen
again?'"

NOTES

"In the Footsteps of Genghis Khan" Genghis Khan was a Mongol conquerer. The Mongols invaded Vietnam three times in the thirteenth century, but were repulsed each time.

Other parts of the poem refer to the French colonization which began in the mid-nineteenth century and continued until 1954, interrupted only by the Japanese military occupation of Vietnam during World War II.

D. F. BROWN

D. F. Brown was born in 1948 in Springfield, Missouri. He served in the United States Army, 1968-77, as a clinical specialist, including service in Vietnam as a medic with B Company, First Battalion, Fourteenth Infantry, Fourth Division. He holds an M.A. from San Francisco State University, where he subsequently taught creative writing. Currently, he is a ward clerk at Alta Bates Hospital in Berkeley, California.

Brown's poetry has appeared in *Transfer, Intervention, Five Fingers Review, Colorado Review, Ironwood, Barque,* and *IF.* He has been anthologized in *Practising Angels, Unwinding the Vietnam War,* and *The Discovery of Poetry.* In addition, Brown has a volume of poetry:

Returning Fire. San Francisco: San Francisco State University Press, 1984.

Coming Home

for Janice Bolton

There is something I want to say
Not anything you need believe
But there is no thunder here
And the silence
Nothing forgives

I march out vagrant
A culprit at home nowhere
Or everywhere
Dancing stealth
Into living rooms

Someone has stacked his books
Records, souvenirs, pretending
This will always be light
And zoned residential

Patrols

This is where stacking pays off.
Invent numbers each time you need one.
Sunlight more than names, any name.
Someplace, he put them—
The days you watch good friends die

The world keeps moving
Hard notes cut light
Limbs branching, the vines
They hold it all together—
Someone says the war is over
"Look how it ended"—the end

What we say for the nights
I could run naked taking hills
From the small dark people

You always hear
How they drag their dead away
And who kept score

Returning Fire

for Bruce Weigl and Ngo Vinh Long

Hell hath no Power over pagans.
This is still life.
          —RIMBAUD

what we think
         we remember
empty
    waiting in the rain
for the last plane
         you know
you were there
        watching
each drop collect dust
         as if getting wet
made a difference
        say the names
take any way back
        down a hot tropic
trail to good soldiers
         slopped in mud
in the ache
       among believers

paint your face green
                and pretend
it's too much
            like summer picnics
something
          the kids want to show you
it happens
          like no one can plan
maybe
        only chance to know bravery
you think so
           they drown in it
you can't tell
          people from weeds
some are wide receivers
                  others hug the ground
the sergeant walks around
              like he's running
for election
       talks of growing
old surviving
       each day
a cold six pack
        the evening news
football season
        ends on Sunday
a woman sings the anthem
             for nothing
the rest cheering
        you bought tickets
you want to
       believe in Cézanne
life underlined
       scored yellow
you remember that part
           you keep going
once to the river
        in spring
every weekend
       through summer
true visitor
      they don't know

the season
> why they sacrificed

the trees for you
> children of real travelers

they brush mornings
> and evening the scar

cut in the west
> small circle from here

sandbagged
> they whisper themselves

dusk in the jungle
> for tongues so pure

and gone to god
> you call them

with a motion
> a little hike

a little while longer
> you want them

to slip from green
> clothes wet boots

with plenty hot water
> you would steam off mud

get them ready for bed
> it isn't night

empty spaces
> or the tropics

green is nothing
> it holds the trees

and stops sky
> it isn't guns

or the ammo
> they sleep on knowing

the other side
> creased

and still white
> they never come back

soaked off into jungle
> they rise only

in the rough
> second growth

that follows

When I Am 19 I Was a Medic

for Lee, who sculpts light

All day I always want to know
the angle, the safest approach.
I want to know the right time
to go in. Who is in front
of me, who is behind.
When the last shots were fired,
what azimuth will get me out,
the nearest landing zone.

Each night I lay out all my stuff:
morphine, bandages at my shoulder,
just below, parallel, my rifle.
I sleep strapped to a .45,
bleached into my fear.
I do this under the biggest tree,
some nights I dig
in saying my wife's name
over and over.

I can tell true stories
from the jungle. I never mention
the fun, our sense of humor
embarrasses me. Something
warped it out of place
and bent I drag it along—
keeping track of time spent,
measure what I think we have left.

Now they tell me something else—
I've heard it all before
sliding through the grass
to get here.

Illumination

no sunrise here   three layers of green
give a day a lime glow   evening lasts five
grey minutes   the dark stays all night
lighting a smoke marks the spot for anybody
everything is a dead giveaway

       the new L T dreams up some movement
he has to see   he is truly possessed
has been crying for his girl   she is all
he needs but a little light in the jungle
will make it   go away   he radios base
crank up the 105s   fire illumination

       a we-know-they-know-where-we-are-at
I hope we don't find them   I've been there
seen the pictures

I Was Dancing Alone in Binh Dinh Province

for John Jacobson

There is an award for this,
a decoration, something
they want us to believe.

All flanks covered, always
the point man steps out,
counts each move glancing
for movement he can shoot.
Next two men pull slack—
spaced five meters any blast
will get only one.

Someone will handle the radio.
Someone will carry Band-Aids.
Someone will have a map, compass

the number—his plumb line ignores the hill,
brown paddies, blue river, shallow
deep—it takes too many
38

helicopters
to get here
I don't trust air
to find the place
less a matter of time
sinks into cramps
an ache   in my gut
I lose track with these guys
how gentle they are
rattles with machine guns

Whoever holds title to this
has a handful
soil hearts move through

Eating the Forest

If I am alive in the morning
then I am alive in the dream
  —RIMBAUD

Background is instrumental
mountains start there
a seven year old could draw this—
highlands angle above paddies
block the valley water
is a curl, brown river, everything
green in two shades—
the darkest fills in
edges, covering heroes, marks
out each stalk rising, the other
catches light in corners
turning heat—we live
with the killing, fight
every war we were
raised to fight
an enemy we couldn't see
music going like crazy
on both sides

we rummaged our hearts
forget words
hum the tune

It all depends on forty men
automatic rifles
grenades
faces painted green—
the man behind me is twenty feet away
circles join us, sandbagged
mines point from the spot
we guard with our lives
I keep count for them
the cases—malaria,
hepatitis, VD, purple
hearts, red marks,
red marks we live
soak off into jungle
every day each man
the small, white antimalarial pill
fifty-two Mondays the big orange tablet
I have to go on
nothing got to die

We were killing ourselves
uphill
a trail to the ridge
through jungle
uphill
there was no noise
even the birds keep quiet
uphill
the trail through
no noise, we were
jungle, birds
the ridge
uphill
no one would fall

jungle
hills with their numbers
valleys with names

We think we are
ready awake
all night the dead
snap back on legs
they had the day before
bleached into dreams
we talk sweet for them
working their slow way around
new at being dead, young
and nervous kick
the dirt, try wiping
off mud, and still
they carry everything—
ammo, the charges, flares
cut sharp floating
angles, they don't kill
shadows, we are cut-outs,
the dead stay for contrast
each one on point
calling out code
for his presence
they don't need music
days have no names
the 10,000 versions
of the war are one
in the great, late All-Night
they keep track in our sleep
—visibility
far off standing
light thick sound
tracked each flash
crosses soldiers,
trained to sleep
where the moon sinks
and bring the darkness home

Still Later There Are War Stories

For those who think of us, not as we were
—RANDALL JARRELL

1

Another buddy dead.
There is enough dying—
Gary Cooper will
ride up, slow and easy
slide off his horse
without firing a shot
save us all.

It is a matter of waiting.
We grow old counting the year
in days, one by one
each morning ritual marks
one more, one less—
the plane has yet to land.

2

Down freeways, past federal cemetery flags
half masted, dark green lawn,
the watered rows of stone—I could have
come home—November five—to a decade
recounting days since, another
waiting above jungle trails
for then we hope never to see—
field hospital beds, orthopedic surgeons
saving lives, fifteen minutes away. . . .

Daily boy scout excursions
through brush so thick
one hour hacking brings you
twenty feet closer to home,
down a new tropic trail. The jungle
loaded, nobody
comes away in one piece.

First Person—1981

there are days I have to pretend
I am someone else to get out of bed
make all the necessary noises
remember how it ended, how the end
is still caught in so many

I get through these days
the lowest part of the jungle
a pale green gnarl
roots and vines
searching for sunlight
through
this tangle

Vietnamization

You're in this someplace else you dream
Night a thing, tough shit all over, darkness

You're talking to a guy who picks up the pieces
He tells you he's tired of the hours

Long hours bending, the explosions
Weird dink songs up through the brush

One damn thing for sure, he says, next time
I don't want to run short of the bags

These guys get greased
They're going out like they're supposed to

No more makeshift crap
Some asshole somewhere can afford it

Ain't a bit of fucking funny involved, he says
For a while you don't hear the music

NOTES

"I Was Dancing Alone in Binh Dinh Province"   Binh Dinh was a province of South Vietnam that was heavily supportive of the Viet Cong. The political-geographical structure of Vietnam consisted of provinces, districts, villages, and hamlets in descending order of size and importance.

"Eating the Forest"   The fifty-two Mondays refers to the standard tour of duty served by U.S. army, navy, and air force personnel in Vietnam—one year. United States Marines usually served thirteen months.

MICHAEL CASEY

Michael Casey was born in 1947. He served in the United States Army, 1968-70, including service in Vietnam, 1969-70, as a military policeman with the Americal Division. He holds a B.S. from Lowell Technological Institute, and an M.A.H. from the State University of New York at Buffalo. He has worked as a college instructor, book reviewer, and film critic, and is a recipient of the Yale Series of Younger Poets Award.

Casey's writing has appeared in *The Little Magazine, The Nation, The Bellingham Review, The Nantucket Review*, the *New York Times, Rolling Stone*, and *College English*, and has been anthologized in *Winning Hearts and Minds* and *Vietnam Anthology*. Casey is author, also, of a volume of poetry:

Obscenities. New Haven, Conn.: Yale University Press, 1972.

A Bummer

We were going single file
Through his rice paddies
And the farmer
Started hitting the lead track
With a rake
He wouldn't stop
The TC went to talk to him
And the farmer
Tried to hit him too
So the tracks went sideways
Side by side
Through the guy's fields
Instead of single file
Hard On, Proud Mary
Bummer, Wallace, Rosemary's Baby
The Rutgers Road Runner
And
Go Get Em—Done Got Em
Went side by side
Through the fields
    If you have a farm in Vietnam
And a house in hell
Sell the farm
And go home

Road Hazard

Eddie throws an old poncho
We found on the ruins of LZ Gator
Over most of it
And he grabs
The more solid looking leg
And drags it to the side of the road
I pick up the loose hand
A right hand
That is still warm
Because of the sun
And go to the side of the road
To tuck it
Under the right side
Of the poncho
With my being a Cong Giao
I think of making the sign
Of the cross but don't
Want to appear weak
To my public   the Nuoc Mau
Citizens standing around this scene
Holding their noses
We   Eddie and I
Go back to the jeep
Where Hieu was waiting all this time
With a handkerchief over his nose
I still am having
What poker face I have on
but Hieu still pats me on the shoulder
And says   okay   okay   no sweat   no sweat
And I'm put out that
He doesn't do likewise to Eddie
Maybe I did appear the weakling

The LZ Gator Body Collector

See
Her back is arched
Like something's under it
That's why I thought

It was booby trapped
But it's not
It just must have been
Over this rock here
And somebody moved it
After corpus morta stiffened it
I didn't know it was
A woman at first
I couldn't tell
But then I grabbed
Down there
It's a woman or was
It's all right
I didn't mind
I had gloves on then

For The Old Man

The old man was mumbling
And Delbert was shouting at him
Im! Im! Im!
Until Booboo told Delbert
To shut the fuck up
The old man was skinny
The old man had looked young
With the sand bag
Over his head
Without the bag
The man was old
There was a bump
The size of a grapefruit
On his head
When the bag was taken off
The man
Clasped his hands
In front of him
And bowed to us
Each in turn
To Booboo, Delbert, and me
He kept it up too
He wouldn't stop

His whole body shaking
Shivering with fright
And somehow
With his hands
Clasped before him
It seemed as if
He was praying to us
It made all of us
Americans
Feel strange

Hoa Binh

August thirty-first
Stanley was all excited
She just made eighteen
And got to vote
For the first time
There were sixteen slates
To vote for
In Vietnam that year
And every slate's poster
Said that
That slate
Wanted Hoa Binh
From voting
She came back to me
All excited
Casee
I vote for Hoa Binh
That's nice, Stanley
I did too
Back in Hoa Ky
I hope your vote counts

HORACE COLEMAN

Horace Coleman was born in 1943 in Dayton, Ohio. He served in the United States Air Force, 1965-70, as an air traffic controller/intercept director, including service in Vietnam, 1967-68. He holds a B.A. and an M.F.A. from Bowling Green State University. A former artist-in-residence for the Ohio Arts Council, he has taught creative writing, poetry, composition and Afro-American literature at the university level. He is currently a staff writer for McDonnell Douglas Astronautics.

Coleman's poetry has appeared in *American Poetry Review, Kansas Quarterly, New Letters,* and *In These Times.* He has been anthologized in *From A to Z: 200 Contemporary American Poets; Speak Easy, Speak Free; Demilitarized Zones; Peace Is Our Profession;* and *Leaving the Bough: 50 American Poets for the 80s.* Coleman, has, also, a collection of poetry:

Between a Rock & a Hard Place, in *Four Black Poets.* Kansas City, Mo.: BkMk Press, 1977.

OK Corral East
Brothers in the Nam

Sgt. Christopher and I are
in Khanh Hoi down by the docks
in the Blues Bar where the women
are brown and there is no Saigon Tea
making our nightly HIT—'Hore Inspection Tour
watching the black   digging night sights
  soul sounds   getting tight

the grunts in the corner raise undisturbed hell
the timid white MP has his freckles pale
as he walks past the high dude
in the doorway in his lavender jump-suit
to remind the mama-san quietly of curfew
    he chokes on the weed smoke
    he sees nothing his color here
and he fingers his army rosary his .45

but this is not Cleveland or Chicago
he can't cringe any one here and our
gazes like brown punji stakes impale him

we have all killed something recently
we know who owns the night
and carry darkness with us

Night Flare Drop, Tan Son Nhut

It is Tet
    some Vietnamese excuse for fireworks
and the war sneaks into Saigon
while young girls from villages in the Delta
    who have learned to use make-up and read comic
        books
suck off fat Air Force colonels
    All is joy
Roman candles chase tracers
Little rockets bark at dancing dragons
In the foreign cemetery
    at the entrance to the base
dying soldiers are having a colorful fire fight
Six Vietnamese MPs
                eager to watch
run into a mine field
    and throw yellow confetti for yards
in 100 P Alley the boy pimps laugh
    and sell three-day-old sandwiches
    to Americans afraid to come out of their rooms
For the first time in years no chauffeur-driven
    Mercedes bull through the streets
And trapped in the bar at the Officers' Open Mess
off-duty pilots
            in dirty flight suits
stand in front of the air-conditioners
    sweating
Overhead frightened planes circle
    shedding magnesium tears that
    burn deep holes in the night
But the dark
    like the VC   always comes back

Remembrance of Things Past

mortars are
the devil coughing
napalm?
Baudelaire never had

50

such flowers
such bright fleur de lis
such evil

claymores
shatter more than bones

when they attacked we
killed them dreams and all
we thought

we fired artillery   they
shot hatred back

when we burned their bones
they loathed us still   dying
still trying to get their crisp
black fingers on our white throats

In Ca Mau

in Ca Mau
the women sweep the canal with their oars
on the way to the floating fruit market
bananas
pineapples
grapes with husks stacked in slender sampans
the Americans in Ca Mau eat tin-skinned food
play prostitute roulette clap
                  syph
                  rigid love
with rifles under the bed in Ca Mau

the people race bicycles on Sundays
children play soccer on the parade square
the Americans don't come
pigs walk the streets alone
GIs ride six to a fast jeep

they pacify the forest of U Minh
with five-hundred-pound bombs
that fall five miles and shake

the yellow palm-thatched huts and
the yellowed stucco houses and the
yellow tent O Club of Ca Mau

they hunt communist water buffalo
with quad .50s and infra-red
they scream howitzers at suspicious rice
but one bullet
makes a helicopter a shotgunned duck
one rocket trips the man-blind radar
off its legs and the Americans
leave and the women sweep
after them in Ca Mau

A Black Soldier Remembers

My Saigon daughter I saw only once
standing in the dusty square
across from the Brink's BOQ/PX
in back of the National Assembly
next to the ugly statue of
the crouching marines facing
the fish pond the VC blew up
during Tet.

The amputee beggars watch us.
The same color and the same eyes.
She does not offer me one of the
silly hats she sells Americans and
I have nothing she needs but
the sad smile she already has.

A Downed Black Pilot Learns
How to Fly

"now that the war is over
we'll have to kill each other again
but I'll send my medals to Hanoi
and let them make bullets if
they'll ship my leg back and

if they mail me an ash tray
made from my F4C they can keep
the napalm as a bonus. Next time
I'll wait and see if they've declared
war on me—or just America."

NOTES

"OK Corral East/Brothers in the Nam" The title is a play on the 1957 Hollywood
movie, *Gunfight at the OK Corral.*

W. D. EHRHART

W. D. Ehrhart was born in 1948 in Roaring Spring, Pennsylvania. He served in the United States Marine Corps, 1966-69, including service in Vietnam with First Battalion, First Marines, 1967-68. He holds a B.A. from Swarthmore College and an M.A. from the University of Illinois at Chicago. He is the recipient of an Academy of American Poets Prize, a Mary Roberts Rinehart Foundation Grant, the President's Medal from Veterans for Peace, Inc., and two fellowships from the Pennsylvania Council on the Arts. Currently, he teaches at Germantown Friends School in Philadelphia.

Ehrhart's work has appeared in *American Poetry Review*, *New Letters*, *The Virginia Quarterly Review*, *The Chronicle of Higher Education*, *TriQuarterly*, and *Colorado Review*. He was poetry advisor to the twelve unit high school curriculum *The Lessons of the Vietnam War*, published in 1988 by the Center for Social Studies Education. Ehrhart has authored or edited, in addition, the following volumes:

POETRY

A Generation of Peace. New York: New Voices, 1975.

A Generation of Peace. Rev. ed. San Jose, Calif.: Samisdat, 1977.

Rootless. San Jose, Ca.: Samisdat, 1977.

Empire. Richford, Vt.: Samisdat, 1978.

The Awkward Silence. Stafford, Va.: Northwoods Press, 1980.

The Samisdat Poems. Richford, Vt.: Samisdat, 1980.

Matters of the Heart. Easthampton, Mass.: Adastra Press, 1981.

Channel Fever. Port Jefferson, N.Y.: Backstreet Editions, 1982.

The Outer Banks & Other Poems. Easthampton, Mass.: Adastra Press, 1984.

To Those Who Have Gone Home Tired: New & Selected Poems. New York: Thunder's Mouth Press, 1984.

Winter Bells. Easthampton, Mass.: Adastra Press, 1988.

NONFICTION

Vietnam-Perkasie: A Combat Marine Memoir. Jefferson, N.C.: McFarland, 1983; New York: Zebra Books, 1985.

Going Back: An Ex-Marine Returns to Vietnam. Jefferson, N.C.: McFarland, 1987.

Passing Time: Memoir of a Vietnam Veteran Against the War. Jefferson, N.C.: McFarland, 1989. (Published originally as *Marking Time.* New York: Avon, 1986).

EDITED WORKS

With Jan Barry. *Demilitarized Zones: Veterans after Vietnam.* Perkasie, Pa: East River Anthology, 1976.

With Merritt Clifton. *Those Who Were There: Eyewitness Accounts of the War in Southeast Asia, 1956-1975 & Aftermath.* Paradise, Calif.: Dustbooks, 1984.

Carrying the Darkness. The Poetry of the Vietnam War. Lubbock: Texas Tech University Press, 1989. (Published originally as *Carrying the Darkness: American Indochina—The Poetry of the Vietnam War.* New York: Avon Books, 1985.)

Farmer Nguyen

When we swept through farmer Nguyen's hamlet,
some people said that farmer Nguyen
had given rice to the Vietcong.

You picked the wrong side, farmer Nguyen.
We took you in, and beat you,
and put you in a barbed wire cage.

When the Vietcong returned to farmer Nguyen's hamlet,
some people said that farmer Nguyen
had given information to the Round Eyes.

Wrong again, farmer Nguyen.
They took more rice, and beat you,
and made you carry supplies.

Night Patrol

Another night coats the nose and ears:
smells of fish and paddy water,
smoke from cooking fires and stale urine
drift uneasily, cloaked in silence;
the marketplace deserted, shuttered
houses, empty paths, all cloaked in silence;
shadows bristle.

Our gravel-crunching boots tear great
holes in the darkness, make us wince
with every step. A mangy dog
pits the stomach: rifles level;
nervous fingers hit the safety catch.

The Next Step

The next step you take
may lead you into an ambush.

The next step you take
may trigger a tripwire.

The next step you take
may detonate a mine.

The next step you take
may tear your leg off at the hip.

The next step you take
may split your belly open.

The next step you take
may send a sniper's bullet through your brain.

The next step you take.
The next step you take.

The next step.
The next step.

The next step.

Guerrilla War

It's practically impossible
to tell civilians
from the Vietcong.

Nobody wears uniforms.
They all talk
the same language,
(and you couldn't understand them
even if they didn't).

They tape grenades
inside their clothes,

and carry satchel charges
in their market baskets.

Even their women fight;
and young boys,
and girls.

It's practically impossible
to tell civilians
from the Vietcong;

after a while,
you quit trying.

Hunting

Sighting down the long black barrel,
I wait till front and rear sights
form a perfect line on his body,
then slowly squeeze the trigger.

The thought occurs
that I have never hunted anything in my whole life
except other men.

But I have learned by now
where such thoughts lead,
and soon pass on
to chow, and sleep,
and how much longer till I change my socks.

A Relative Thing

We are the ones you sent to fight a war
you didn't know a thing about.

It didn't take us long to realize
the only land that we controlled
was covered by the bottoms of our boots.

When the newsmen said that naval ships
had shelled a VC staging point,
we saw a breastless woman
and her stillborn child.

We laughed at old men stumbling
in the dust in frenzied terror
to avoid our three-ton trucks.

We fought outnumbered in Hue City
while the ARVN soldiers looted bodies
in the safety of the rear.
The cookies from the wives of Local 104
did not soften our awareness.

We have seen the pacified supporters
of the Saigon government
sitting in their jampacked cardboard towns,
their wasted hands placed limply in their laps,
their empty bellies waiting for the rice
some district chief has sold
for profit to the Vietcong.

We have been Democracy on Zippo raids,
burning houses to the ground,
driving eager amtracs through new-sown fields.

We are the ones who have to live
with the memory that we were the instruments

of your pigeon-breasted fantasies.
We are inextricable accomplices
in this travesty of dreams:
but we are not alone.

We are the ones you sent to fight a war
you did not know a thing about—
those of us that lived
have tried to tell you what went wrong.
Now you think you do not have to listen.

Just because we will not fit
into the uniforms of photographs
of you at twenty-one
does not mean you can disown us.

We are your sons, America,
and you cannot change that.
When you awake,
we will still be here.

Making the Children Behave

Do they think of me now
in those strange Asian villages
where nothing ever seemed
quite human
but myself
and my few grim friends
moving through them
hunched
in lines?

When they tell stories to their children
of the evil
that awaits misbehavior,
is it me they conjure?

To Those Who Have Gone Home Tired

After the streets fall silent
After the bruises and the tear-gassed eyes are healed
After the consensus has returned
After the memories of Kent and My Lai and Hiroshima
lose their power
and their connections with each other
and the sweaters labeled Made in Taiwan
After the last American dies in Canada
and the last Korean in prison
and the last Indian at Pine Ridge
After the last whale is emptied from the sea
and the last leopard emptied from its skin
and the last drop of blood refined by Exxon
After the last iron door clangs shut
behind the last conscience
and the last loaf of bread is hammered into bullets
and the bullets
scattered among the hungry

What answers will you find
What armor will protect you
when your children ask you

Why?

Letter

to a North Vietnamese soldier
whose life crossed paths with mine
in Hue City, February 5th, 1968

Thought you killed me
with that rocket? Well, you nearly did:
splattered walls and splintered air,
knocked me cold and full of holes,
and brought the roof down on my head.

But I lived,
long enough to wonder often

how you missed; long enough
to wish too many times
you hadn't.

What's it like back there?
It's all behind us here;
and after all those years of possibility,
things are back to normal.
We just had a special birthday,
and we've found again our inspiration
by recalling where we came from
and forgetting where we've been.

Oh, we're still haggling over pieces
of the lives sticking out
beyond the margins of our latest
history books—but no one haggles
with the authors.

Do better than that
you cockeyed gunner with the brass
to send me back alive among a people
I can never feel
at ease with anymore:

remember where you've been, and why.
And then build houses; build villages,
dikes and schools, songs
and children in that green land
I blackened with my shadow
and the shadow of my flag.

Remember Ho Chi Minh
was a poet: please,
do not let it all come down
to nothing.

A Confirmation

for Gerry Gaffney

Solemn Douglas firs stride slowly
down steep hills to drink
the waters of the wild Upper Umqua.
In a small clearing in the small
carved ravine of a feeder stream
we camp, pitching our tent
in the perfect stillness of the shadows
of the Klamath Indians. Far off,
almost in a dream, the logging trucks
growl west down through the mountains
toward the mills in Roseburg.

I hold the stakes, you hammer:
"Watch the fingers!"—both laughing.
Both recall, in easy conversation,
one-man poncho-tents rigged
side by side in total darkness,
always you and I, in iron heat,
in the iron monsoon rains—
not like this at all; and yet,
though years have passed
and we are older by a lifetime,
a simple slip of thought, a pause,
and here: nothing's changed.

For we were never young, it seems;
not then, not ever. I couldn't even cry
the day you went down screaming, angry
jagged steel imbedded in your knee—
I knew you would live,
and I knew you wouldn't be back,
and I was glad, and a little jealous.
Two months later I went down.

We all went down eventually,
the villages aflame, the long
grim lines of soldiers, flotsam
in the vortex of a sinking illusion:

goodbye, Ginny; goodbye, John Kennedy;
goodbye, Tom Paine and high school history—
though here we are still, you and I.
We live our lives now
in a kind of awkward silence
in the perfect stillness of the shadows
of the Klamath Indians.

And I am truly happy
to be with you again. We stand
on the rocks; you point to clear
patches between white water
where the shadows of sleek fish slip,
effortless streaks of energy.
I'm clumsy: with an old, eager patience
you teach me how to cast the fly
gently, so it rides on the surface
with the current, far downstream—
till the rod bends, springs back,
bends again: strike! Your excitement
rises above the river like a wild
song the Douglas firs bend
imperceptibly to hear: shouts,
advice, encouragement, half an hour
and a fourteen-inch rainbow trout
panting hard, eyes alive, its tiny heart
beating with defiance still unbroken
though I hold the fish
helpless in my hands.

I throw the fish back
in the awkward silence, and you
slip your arm around my shoulders
gently for a moment, knowing why.

Later we eat from cans,
the rainbow flashing in the fire
reflecting in our eyes, alive:
familiar gestures—fingers burned
by hot tin lids, a mild curse, quiet
laughter, swish of a knifeblade
plunging idly deep into damp earth.

You ask do I remember the little shy
flower who always wore a white *ao dai*,
and I smile across the flames as the river
tumbles through the darkness toward the sea
that laps the shores of Asia.

The wind moves through the Douglas firs,
and in the perfect stillness of the shadows
of the Klamath Indians, we test
our bonds and find them, after all
these years, still sound—knowing
in the awkward silence we will always share
something worth clinging to
out of the permanent past of stillborn dreams:
the ancient, implacable wisdom
of ignorance shattered forever, a new
reverence we were never taught
by anyone we believed, a frail hope
we gave each other, communion
made holy by our shame.

You've found religion since then,
a wife, and two children;
I write poems you admire.
The knee's still stiff, like an old
high school football wound,
and I have trouble hearing. We are
both tired, but reluctant to sleep:
both understand we will never
see each other again; once is enough.
The logging trucks have long since
left the mountains in peace;
in the perfect stillness, we can almost
hear the solemn Douglas firs drinking
the waters of the wild Upper Umqua
we have come so far to worship:
together now, in this small circle of light,
we bow our hearts to the shadows
of the Klamath Indians; now,
and always, in our need.

The Blizzard of Sixty-Six

Snow came early here, and hard:
roads treacherous; wires down.
School authorities should have cancelled
the annual high school Christmas dance:
two couples died on the way home.
"Tragedy," the local papers declared,
but the snow kept falling.

Somewhere in a folder in a file
is a photograph of me in a uniform:
one stripe for PFC; girl in a yellow gown.
I took her home through the falling snow,
kissed goodnight, and left for Asia.

All through that long year, snow
fell and fell on the green rice,
on gray buffalo, thatched huts, green
patrols, and the mounting yellow dead.

Randy, class of '65, died
in terminal cold in the Mekong Delta;
Kenny, class of '66, died in a blizzard
of lead in the Central Highlands;
I came home with permanent chills,
the yellow nameless dead of Asia
crammed into my seabag, and all of us
looking for a reason.

We never found one. Presidents
come and go away like snowdrifts
in driveways; generals come and go;
the earth goes on silently turning
and turning through its seasons,
and the snow keeps falling.

Twice Betrayed

for Nguyen Thi My Huong
Ho Chi Minh City
December 1985

Some American soldier
came to your mother for love,
or lust, a moment's respite from loneliness,
and you happened. Fourteen years later,
I meet you on the street at night
in the city that was once called Saigon,
and you are almost a woman,
barefooted, dressed in dirty clothes,
beautiful with your one shy dimple.

It doesn't really matter who won;
either way, you were always destined
to be one of the losers:
if he wasn't killed, your father left
for the place we used to call The World
years before the revolution's tanks
crushed the gates of the old regime forever.

Now we sit on a bench in a crowded park
burdened by history. It isn't easy
being here again after all these years.
I marvel at your serenity—but of course,
you can't possibly know who I am,
or how far I have come to be here.
You only know that I look like you,
that together we are outcasts.

And so we converse in gestures and signs
and the few words we can both understand,
and for now it almost seems enough
just to discover ways to make you smile.

But it isn't, and I have no way
to tell you that I cannot stay here
and I cannot take you with me.
I will tell my wife about you.

I will put your photograph on my desk.
I will dream you are my own daughter.
But none of that will matter
when you come here tomorrow
and I'm gone.

NOTES

"To Those Who Have Gone Home Tired" The first few lines refer to the street demonstrations of the late 1960s and early 1970s.

In May 1970, four students were killed and nine others wounded by Ohio National Guard troops during a demonstration at Kent State University to protest the United States-South Vietnamese invasion of Cambodia. No one was ever charged in the shootings.

United States Army troops massacred a large number of Vietnamese civilians (estimates run between 100 and 500) at a place called My Lai in April 1968. Lt. William Calley was eventually found guilty of twenty-two counts of murder, but all others charged (both Calley's troops and his superiors) were found not guilty.

Hiroshima was the first city against which nuclear weapons were used.

During the war, many young American men sought asylum in Canada rather than submitting to involuntary military service and possible service in Vietnam. A smaller number of military personnel, some of them already Vietnam veterans, also fled to Canada.

The Republic of Korea (South Korea) has been a major United States ally and client since the Korean War, but the policies of the various Korean governments since the 1950s have often been extremely repressive.

In 1974, members of the American Indian Movement clashed with agents of the Federal Bureau of Investigation at Pine Ridge Reservation in South Dakota.

"A Relative Thing" The title is a play on the adage, "You can always choose your friends, but you can't choose your relatives."

While the end of the poem refers to America's "sons," as many as 15,000 women also served in Vietnam in various military and civilian capacities. Eight women are among the names on the wall of the Vietnam Veterans Memorial in Washington, D.C.

"Letter" The "special birthday" refers to the U.S. Bicentennial in 1976.

Ho Chi Minh, by far the most dominant figure in Vietnam's struggle for independence during the 20th century, was president of the Democratic Republic of Vietnam from its founding in 1945 until his death in 1969. He was also an accomplished poet.

"Twice Betrayed" There is a dramatic and famous photograph showing North Vietnamese tanks breaking down the gates of the Presidential Palace in Saigon on April 30th, 1975.

BRYAN ALEC FLOYD

Bryan Alec Floyd was born in 1940 in Oklahoma City, Oklahoma. He served in the United States Marine Corps, 1966-68, as a chaplain's assistant. He holds a B.A. from Seattle University and an M.A. from Johns Hopkins University and has received a Johns Hopkins Writing Seminars Fellowship, a State University of New York Professor's Writing Grant, and a Pulitzer Prize nomination. Currently, he teaches at State University of New York, Suffolk County Community College.

Floyd's poetry has appeared in *Beloit Poetry Journal*, *Voices International*, *Hyacinths & Biscuits*, and the *New York Times* and has been anthologized in *The Lessons of the Vietnam War* and *Vietnam Anthology*. In addition, Floyd has two volumes of poetry:

The Long War Dead. New York: Avon Books, 1976; Sag Harbor, N.Y.: The Permanent Press, 1983.
Prayerfully Sinning. Sag Harbor, N.Y.: The Permanent Press, 1984.

Private Ian Godwin, U.S.M.C.

He stepped on a land mine,
falling up instead of down.
Afterward he lay still, listening
to his feet get up without him
and slowly walk away.
For this he was given a medal,
which he swallowed.
He was given crutches,
which he burned.
Flown Med-Evac to San Diego,
he was ordered to rehabilitate.
But he started to salute bedpans
and give orders to hypos,
and tell catheters to "Fire!"
He stood on his stumps,
yelling that he was going
to chase daisies up the hills
because winter had greened into spring,
that God had become rain and it was raining,
the soft mud of Vietnam cool between his toes.

Sergeant Brandon Just, U.S.M.C.

He was alive with death:
Her name was Sung
and she was six years old.
By slightest mistake of degrees
on an artillery azimuth,
he had called for rockets and napalm.
Their wild wizardry of firepower
expired her mistake of a village,
killing everyone except her,
and napalm made her look
like she was dead among the dead,
she alone alive among their upturned corpses
burning toward the sky.
He and the platoon
got to them too late,
removing only her
to a hospital inside his base, Da Nang.
In the months that followed,
when he could make it back from the boonies,
he always went to visit Sung.
Finally he was ordered to a desk job at the base.
He visited her every day,
though he accused himself of being alive
and would stand in a slump,
breathing his despair,
before entering the children's ward.
But he would enter.
Sung, knowing it was him,
would turn toward the sound of his feet,
her own, seared beyond being feet,
crisply trying to stand on shadows,
cool but unseen.
And as he would come in,
Sung would hobble up to him
in her therapeutic cart,
smiling even when she did not smile, lipless,
her chin melted to her chest
that would never become breasts.
He would stand
and wait for her touch upon his hand

with her burn-splayed fingers
that came to lay a fire upon his flesh.
Sung was alive
and would live on despite life,
but even now her skull
seemed to be working its way through
the thin, fragile solids of wasted, waxen skin.
Her head was as bald as a bomb
whose paint had peeled.
She had no nose
and her ears were gone.
Her eyes had been removed,
and because they were not there,
they were there
invisibly looking him through.
Sung was child-happy
that he came and cared,
and when he would start to leave,
she would agonize her words
out of the hollow that was her mouth.
Her tongue, bitten in two while she had burned,
strafing his ears,
saying, without mercy,
I love you.

Corporal Charles Chungtu, U.S.M.C.

This is what the war ended up being about:
we would find a V.C. village,
and if we could not capture it
or clear it of Cong,
we called for jets.
The jets would come in, low and terrible,
sweeping down, and screaming,
in their first pass over the village.
Then they would return, dropping their first bombs
that flattened the huts to rubble and debris.
And then the jets would sweep back again
and drop more bombs
that blew the rubble and debris
to dust and ashes.

And then the jets would come back once again,
in a last pass, this time to drop napalm
that burned the dust and ashes to just nothing.
Then the village
that was not a village any more
was our village.

Lance Corporal Purdue Grace, U.S.M.C.

He went home when the new replacements arrived,
but before he left
he talked with several of them,
all of whom looked scared and a bit self-pitying.
They knew he had made it through his tour
without getting a cold much less a wound.
One of the braver replacements
told him they were all terrified.
The Lance Corporal told them, "To be scared is okay.
I've seen lots of men change their pants
more than once a day, they were so scared.
But don't expect sympathy.
Sympathy is a sad word found in the dictionary
somewhere between scab and syphilis.
Always remember to keep your head out of your ass
and your ass out of the air.
Know this about this fucked-up war
that will never unfuck itself—
Life in Vietnam is a sea of shit:
Some people sink.
Some people swim.
And some people go in boats."

Private Jack Smith, U.S.M.C.

Since he came back
he never met with the friends he fought with in Nam
and never mentioned the war:
Once he was ordered out
of his five-man fire team
to go and be point man.

He was about a hundred feet up front
when someone in his fire team
tripped a land mine,
and whoever it had been,
along with the other three,
were left somehow
unreasonably alive—just.
And there had been a Lance Corporal in his squad
whom the threat of peace always made aggressive.
The Lance Corporal was a sniper
with twenty-six kills marked up.
The Private was with him
when the Lance Corporal was cut down by a V.C. sniper,
and as the Private held him,
the Lance Corporal held his intestines in his hands,
saying, "I don't want to die. I'm afraid to die."
And died.
One night the Private and two other guys
slept in a sandbagged hootch
that was hit by two direct mortar rounds,
he being blasted awake and away
without a scratch
while those other two
were just pieces of themselves.
He could not find their heads
but laid the rest to rest
in ponchos that no one could tag
because their remains were Officially Unidentifiable.
After that he decided
to avoid moderation at any extreme
and shot every anything that moved.
He came to think that his officers
were more concerned with rank and medals
than with the lives and deaths of their men.
He came to feel that his politicians were garbage
who should have been wasted.
When he finished his tour of duty
and was sent home and Honorably Discharged,
he decided to live with his parents
and began college,
and majored in History on the GI Bill.
He thought he might join the peace movement

and started going to rallies.
His college was shut down four times
the semester he started,
and during the fourth shutdown,
his college president was beaten up
by several anti-imperalists
who took over the college
and burned down the ROTC building
and the library
and who kept the president in his office
until he resigned, on his own accord of course.
But the ex-Private kept going to the rallies,
looked, listened, learned.
He got to thinking
that most of the rally speakers
were happy with hallucinations,
and he thought
that several of the tens of thousands
in the crowds who kept yelling Right On
had either forgotten, or had never known,
that absolutism is addictive
and that the mob, any mob for any cause,
is always
pregnant with fascism.
The fifth time his college was shut down
by the anti-imperialist anti-
fascists,
he knew what he knew,
and knew that he must try
to walk through and beyond the mob
which had blocked his way to History.
He tried, knowing they would beat hell out of him,
and they did.
But it was he who was arrested
for disturbing the peace.
He was jailed.
His dad bailed him out
and told him he hoped he was satisfied
and that he should have felt ashamed.
But instead, the ex-Private felt himself feel nothing.
He went home again, and packed, and left.
That was four years ago.
Nobody has heard from him since.

Captain James Leson, U.S.M.C.

His corpse was returned
to the U.S. in March, 1974, from Hanoi,
where the criminal Captain had been
a prisoner from 1967 until his natural death in 1973.
An official spokesman
of the Peoples' Republic of North Vietnam
related with regrets
that the bourgeois elitist officer
had confessed to having been a lackey
for the war-mongering capitalists
and their running dogs, the South Vietnamese.
The official spokesman said
the aristocratic officer, without being intimidated,
had confessed that he had enjoyed killing innocent children
and had loved watching cities and villages burn.
And that before the imperialist Captain had naturally died,
he had written his regrets and spoken them over the radio
that his sins and the sins of his mafia nation
could have been avoided
had he been as brave as a Rennie Davis or a Jane Fonda
and his country as committed to fighting inequality and racism
as the governments of Sweden and India.
Enough said,
he said before he died his natural death.

Corporal Kevin Spina, U.S.M.C.

He came of a sharecrop farm family
and could barely read and write.
He had never thought
about teaching his heart war.
When he personally received
a letter from the President
of the United States of America
he simply went, having faith.
He put on his uniform
and disappeared
and became his uniform.
When he came back in a box,

he was buried with full military honors,
his family given the flag
that draped his coffin.
Now that flag flies every day
in front of his house.
When the neighbors' children pass by
they always look at that flag
and they always say,
"Someday there will be another war,
and I'm going to be a Marine."

Private First Class Brooks Morgenstein, U.S.M.C.

Her remembered frailty had strengthened his.
His soul was alive for her.
What kept him going
when he would bag and tag bodies
or when out on a search-and-destroy
were her eyes as soft as breasts.
He wanted to write his wife naked words
that would have been more naked when read.
He had chosen the goal of his groin
and it was to grieve,
for his want of her was like pain.
His loneliness and lust were his and he theirs
during every second of these thirteen months.
He only knew as he held his rifle
during a sweeping operation
that next year he would hold her,
and when he kissed her,
his tongue would touch hers
and she would feel
as though a piece of the sun
was in her mouth.
When someone in his platoon
was sent back in pieces, alive or dead,
he tried not to despair of heaven,
but sometimes he had faith only in flesh
and would think of her thighs
and remember God.

The heat of the jungle
had pared him thin as peace.
His head was shaven squabby bald.
His uniform clung to him like a huge wet sock,
and he stank of leeches and mud and malaria and fear.
Yet he was all he had,
and his heart would leave him, and long to her heart,
she who had been shy to yield, but had yielded.
The sun in the boonies gloomed everything
with its yellowed heat for air,
but he breathed her fingers.
And her young woman's youngest breasts
suckled his terror,
while her mouth held off boredom
from shattering him insane.
Under a rocket barrage at Khe Sanh,
he once dreamed of her lying open as a wound,
and as raw,
and he had salved and bandaged her
with his mouth and fingers.
During the bad times,
such as when the platoon was ordered to torch a village,
he would feel his rage deepening,
without bottoming out,
and he would be shaking with fear and shame and ecstasy
that he was still alive.
He would make himself think of her,
and with the thirst that comes from drinking of it,
his lust would grow and become exalted
like a great tree,
and he knew if he made it back
she could climb his body
and that he with branches would cover her with himself
and they would be unable to tell
how much of him was him
and how much of him was her.

NOTES

"Captain James Leson, U.S.M.C." Rennie Davis and Jane Fonda were highly visible leaders of the antiwar movement in the United States during the Vietnam war.

"Private First Class Brooks Morgenstein, U.S.M.C." Thirteen months refers to the standard tour of duty in Vietnam served by United States Marines. Army, navy, and air force personnel usually served twelve months.

YUSEF KOMUNYAKAA

Yusef Komunyakaa was born in 1947 in Bogalusa, Louisiana. He served in the United States Army, 1968-71, as an information specialist, including service in Vietnam, 1969-70. He holds a B.A. from the University of Colorado, an M.A. from Colorado State University, and an M.F.A. from the University of California at Irvine. The recipient of the San Francisco Poetry Center Award as well as fellowships from the Fine Arts Work Center in Provincetown, the Louisiana Arts Commission, and the National Endowment for the Arts, he teaches currently in the writing program at Indiana University.

Komunyakaa's poetry has appeared in *Black Warrior Review*, *Cincinnati Review*, *Colorado Review*, *Ironwood*, *Kayak*, *New Orleans Review*, *North American Review*, and *Ploughshares*. In addition, Komunyakaa has authored five volumes of poetry and co-edited an anthology:

Lost in the Bonewheel Factory. Amherst, Mass.: Lynx House Press, 1978.
Copacetic. Middletown, Conn.: Wesleyan University Press, 1984.
Toys in a Field. New Orleans: Black River Press, 1986.
I Apologize for the Eyes in My Head. Middletown, Conn.: Wesleyan University Press, 1986.
Dien Cai Dau. Middletown, Conn.: Wesleyan University Press, 1988.
With Sascha Feinstein. *The Jazz Poetry Anthology*. Bloomington: Indiana University Press. Forthcoming.

Somewhere near Phu Bai

The moon cuts through
night trees like a circular saw
white hot. In the guardshack
I lean on the sandbags,
taking aim at whatever.
Hundreds of blue-steel stars
cut a path, fanning out
silver for a second. If anyone's
there, don't blame me.

I count the shapes ten meters
out front, over & over, making sure
they're always there.
I don't dare blink an eye.
The white-painted backs
of the Claymore mines
like quarter-moons.

They say Victor Charlie will
paint the other sides & turn
the blast toward you.

If I hear a noise
will I push the button
& blow myself away?
The moon grazes treetops.
I count the Claymores again.
Thinking about buckshot
kneaded in the plastic C-4
of the brain, counting
sheep before I know it.

Starlight Scope Myopia

Gray-blue shadows lift
shadows onto an ox cart.

Making night work for us,
the starlight scope brings
men into killing range.

The river under Vi Bridge
takes the heart away

like the Water God
riding his dragon.
Smoke-colored

Viet Cong
move under our eyelids,

lords over loneliness
winding like coral vine through
sandalwood & lotus,

inside our lowered heads
years after this scene

ends. The brain closes
down. What looks like
one step into the trees,

they're lifting crates of ammo
& sacks of rice, swaying

under their shared weight.
Caught in the infrared,
what are they saying?

Are they talking about women
or calling the Americans

beaucoup dien cai dau?
One of them is laughing.
You want to place a finger

to his lips & say "shhhh."
You try reading ghost talk

on their lips. They say
"up-up we go," lifting as one.
This one, old, bowlegged,

you feel you could reach out
& take him into your arms. You

peer down the sights of your M-16,
seeing the full moon
loaded on an ox cart.

A Break from the Bush

The South China Sea
drives in another herd.
The volleyball's like a punchingbag:
Clem's already lost a tooth
& Johnny's left eye is swollen shut.
Frozen airlifted steaks burn
on a wire grill, & miles away

machineguns can be heard.
Pretending we're somewhere else,
we play harder.
Lee Otis, the point man,
high on Buddha grass,
buries himself up to his neck
in sand. "Can you see me now?
In this spot they gonna
build a Hilton. Invest in Paradise.
Bang, bozos! You're dead."
Frenchie's cassette player
unravels Hendrix's *Purple Haze*.
Snake, 17, from Daytona,
sits at the water's edge,
the ash on his cigarette
pointing to the ground
like a crooked finger. CJ,
who in three days will trip
a fragmentation mine,
runs after the ball
into the whitecaps,
laughing.

Prisoners

Usually at the helipad
I see them stumble-dance
across the hot asphalt
with crokersacks over their heads,
moving toward the interrogation huts,
thin-framed as box kites
of sticks & black silk
anticipating a hard wind
that'll tug & snatch them
out into space. I think
some must be laughing
under their dust-colored hoods,
knowing rockets are aimed
at Chu Lai—that the water's
evaporating & soon the nail
will make contact with metal.

How can anyone anywhere love
these half-broken figures
bent under the sky's brightness?
The weight they carry
is the soil we tread night & day.
Who can cry for them?
I've heard the old ones
are the hardest to break.
An arm twist, a combat boot
against the skull, a .45
jabbed into the mouth, nothing
works. When they start talking
with ancestors faint as camphor
smoke in pagodas, you know
you'll have to kill them
to get an answer.
Sunlight throws
scythes against the afternoon.
Everything's a heat mirage; a river
tugs at their slow feet.
I stand alone & amazed,
with a pill-happy doorgunner
signaling for me to board the Cobra.
I remember how one day
I almost bowed to such figures
walking toward me, under
a corporal's ironclad stare.
I can't say why.
From a half-mile away
trees huddle together,
& the prisoners look like
marionettes hooked to strings of light.

The Dead at Quang Tri

Captain Gungho, my men
are getting real jumpy.
Those we kill get up from
our ambushes & walk away.
We search trees. Like bygones,
if only they'd be done with,

the body counts would mean
something. But this is
harder than counting shadows
of shadows & stones along paths
going nowhere, the way a tiger
circles & backtracks by
smelling its blood on the ground.
The one kneeling beside the pagoda,
remember him? Captain, we won't
talk about that. The Buddhist boy
at the gate with the shaven head
we rubbed for luck
glides by like a white moon.
He won't stay dead, dammit!
Blades aim for the family jewels,
the grass we walk on
won't stay down.

After the Fall

An afternoon storm has hit
the Pearl of the Orient
& stripped nearly everybody.
Bandoliers, miniskirts, tennis shoes,
fatigue jackets, combat boots—
city colors are bruised & polyester
suits limp down sidestreets.
Even the ragpicker is glad
to let his Australian bush hat
with the red feather float away.

Something deeper than sadness
litters the alleys like the insides
kicked out of pillows.
The old mama-san who always
collected scraps of yellow paper,
cigarette butts & matchsticks
through field-stripped years
hides under her cardboard box.
Cowboys park new Harleys
along Lam Son Square

& disappear with gold in their mouths.
Dzung leaves the Continental Hotel
in a newspaper dress.
Hoping for a hard rain,
she moves through broken colors
flung to the ground,
mixing up the words to Trinh's
"Mad Girl's Love Song"
& "Stars Fell on Alabama,"
trying to bite off her tongue.

Boat People

After midnight they load up.
A hundred shadows move about blindly.
Something closer than sleep
hides low voices drifting
toward a red horizon. Tonight's
a black string, the moon's pull—
this boat's headed somewhere.
Lucky to have gotten past
searchlights low-crawling the sea,
like a woman shaking water
from her long dark hair.

Twelve times in three days
they've been lucky,
clinging to each other in gray mist.
Now Thai fishermen gaze out across
the sea as it changes color,
hands shading their eyes
the way sailors do,
minds on robbery & rape.
Sunlight burns blood-orange.

Storm warnings crackle on a radio.
The Thai fishermen turn away.
Not enough water for the trip.
The boat people cling to each other,
faces like yellow sea grapes,
wounded by doubt & salt.

Dusk hangs over the water.
Sea sick, they daydream Jade Mountain
a whole world away, half-drunk
on what they hunger to become.

Thanks

Thanks for the tree
between me & a sniper's bullet.
I don't know what made the grass
sway seconds before the Viet Cong
raised his soundless rifle.
Some voice always followed,
telling me which foot
to put down first.
Thanks for deflecting the ricochet
against that anarchy of dusk.
I was back in San Francisco
wrapped up in a woman's wild colors,
causing some dark bird's love call
to be shattered by daylight
when my hands reached up
& pulled a branch away
from my face. Thanks
for the vague white flower
that pointed to the gleaming metal
reflecting how it is to be broken
like mist over the grass,
as we played some deadly
game for blind gods.
What made me spot the monarch
writhing on a single thread
tied to a farmer's gate,
holding the day together
like an unfingered guitar string,
is beyond me. Maybe the hills
grew weary & leaned a little in the heat.
Again, thanks for the dud
hand grenade tossed at my feet
outside Chu Lai. I'm still
falling through its silence.

I don't know why the intrepid
sun touched the bayonet,
but I know that something
stood among those lost trees
& moved only when I moved.

NOTES

"Boat People"   The title refers to Vietnamese who fled Vietnam at and after the end
of the war. There were two major waves of boat people—1975 and 1978-79, though
the exodus continues to this day. Many of the refugee boats were attacked by
fishermen-pirates from Thailand.

GERALD McCARTHY

Gerald McCarthy was born in 1947 in Endicott, New York. He served in the United States Marine Corps, 1965-68, including service in Vietnam, 1966-67. The recipient of a New York State Creative Artists in Public Service Fellowship in poetry and a New York State Council on the Arts Artists-in-Residence Fellowship, he attended the University of Iowa. He has taught writing at Attica Prison and in migrant labor camps and is currently assistant professor of English at St. Thomas Aquinas College.

McCarthy's writing has appeared in *New Letters, Ploughshares, TriQuarterly, Ohio Review, Mid-American Review, Wisconsin Review,* and *The National Catholic Reporter.* He has been anthologized in *Demilitarized Zones* and *The Lessons of the Vietnam War.* McCarthy's poetry has been published in a volume, also:

War Story. Trumansburg, N.Y.: The Crossing Press, 1977.

War Story
[Excerpts]

1 Med Building

They brought the dead
in helicopters and trucks
and tried to piece the bodies back together,
shoved them in plastic bags
to be sent home.
Sometimes there was an arm or leg
leftover,
it lay around until the next shipment;
they made it fit in somewhere.

7

Flares in a night sky
lighting up the place
like a football field.
Ammo belts
strung over shoulders,
I remember the time
I was a newsboy
with the sunday morning papers,
throwing the headlines.

8

We found him
his chest torn open,
shirt sticky brown.
A corporal with a bayonet
cut off his ears,
and kicked the body
in passing.

9

They shot the woman in the arm,
four of them
raped her
and killed an old man
who tried to interfere;
and later killed the woman too.
She was the enemy.

11

Hot sun,
I walk into a whorehouse
pay the girl
unbuckle my pants
and screw her
sweat sticking to my fatigues
small legs grasping my back
her eyes look up at me
as I come.
Outside the tin-roofed hut
another GI waits his turn.

12

That night in the bunker,
we shared some smoke
and stared out at the stars.
Then,
the mortars blasted
choking sulfur
shoving the magazines in
round after round
deaf,
blinded,
hugging the dirt,

I pissed my pants.
Later,
confusion gone,
you all shot to shit,
you black bastard.
Fuck.

14

   In the early morning the working party
came and filled in the remains of the bunker
with sand. The bodies had been removed
the night before, but the stench lingered.
Soon the earth was worn down smooth by
the boots of the soldiers. They moved off
to build another bunker along the line.
   Clinging to a bush was a dirty piece of
utility jacket. A breeze was blowing in off
the ocean. It rattled the pop cans on the
concertina wire and made hollow, tinny
noises.

17

Well, I said, I came back.
Grandpa pulled the hat down over his eyes
smiled at me in his sleep.
They asked if I wanted breakfast,
some coffee maybe?
Had it been a long ride?
My father looked older.
I smoked a cigarette,
watched the shadows leave the backyard
back into the old house,
my stepmother's chatter,
the old man's sadness
so early in the morning.

19

John Bradt said, It'll be all right
when he gets home.

The farmers in Hale valley are waiting
for the sun to rise.
The train winds slowly

through the mountains.
A voice of strangers
knocking politely
on doors.
The soldiers are coming home,
they carry the sadness with them
like others carry groceries
or clothes in from the line.
There is no music in the parade;
the sound of their coming
waits at the bottoms of rivers,
stones rubbing against each other
in the current.

Arrival

There it is again
the roll of cars in wet streets
hours crushed together in the rain.

I come back to the voices
to their eyes
to a hand turning up a collar in the crowd
to a dark street in the snow.

I lower myself back
my feet in doorways
silence like a rope behind me.

Yes, this must be the right street
and they must be my friends
the stares buttoned to their lapels.
I follow them all the way.

This is where I wanted to get off
in a new winter
on this avenue of trees
the sound of wings

and the wind
wrapping itself around me.

The same glow in windows
and my hands on the hours
on the empty glasses.
The days stuffed in my pocket
like old addresses
and my coat too thin
for this cold.

Finding the Way Back

Morning.
Two sparrows sit on the tin roof
puffing themselves up
like old men in a park.
The longest war of this century
refuses to be ended.
I watch them signing their peace
with twelve different pens
live on t.v.

I remember the ocean
the breeze off the water
sunlight through the curtains of rain.
The young men running
darkness falling around their shoulders.
The children gone
their hearts in open throats.
The faces
the last columns of smoke
tearing the pages from my eyes.

There was never anything to come back to.
Aubrey knew it at Binh San
under the afternoon sun
staring into death.
My brother
I went on living.
There was nothing else
I could do.

The Sound of Guns

1

The sparrow hawk drops to the cornfield
and in the same motion rises.
December's cold tightens around me,
a spider's web frozen white against the glass.

All day the sky is bleak with the coming snow,
the hours seem to pause like the bird
caught in an uplift of wind.
Out back the hay lies in rolls
the cows huddled together near the water troughs.

The highway runs past the brown fields
all the way west to Omaha, and just keeps going.
At the university in town
tight-lipped men tell me the war in Vietnam is over,
that my poems should deal with other things:
earth, fire, water, air.

2

A friend told me once
that ours was a generation of love;
and I know he meant that this was a generation
that took too much, that turned from one death
to another.

I don't know what it is that's kept me going.
At nineteen I stood at night and watched
an airfield mortared. A plane that was to take
me home, burning; men running out of the flames.

Seven winters have slipped away,
the war still follows me.
Never in anything have I found
a way to throw off the dead.

The Fall of Da Nang

Tonight the newspapers report
the air-lift evacuation of Da Nang has failed;
that South Vietnamese soldiers shot their way
through crowds of civilians
to board the last plane that landed.

Years have passed since Aubrey and I
got high together, watching the night sky
across the South China Sea.
Near Monkey Mountain the Viet-Cong are entrenched
hitting the airfield with artillery fire.

I think back to an evening in July
in that same city, when I waited for a plane
to get me out.
My friends watch television.

I pry open the window, listen to the noise
of a passing car on the wet road.
The news interrupts a commercial
with a special bulletin. I watch the faces
of Vietnamese children: the same tired faces
that will always be there.

My friends leave to play poker:
nickel, dime, quarter, they say.
I smoke cigarettes, drink beer.
It's Saturday night, the end of March.

The Hooded Legion

Let us put up a monument to the lie.
—Joseph Brodsky

There are no words here
to witness why we fought,
who sent us or what we hoped to gain.

There is only the rain
as it streaks the black stone,
these memories of rain
that come back to us—
a hooded legion reflected in a wall.

Tonight we wander weaponless and cold
along this shore of the Potomac
like other soldiers who camped here
looking out over smoldering fires into the night.

What did we dream of
the summer before we went away?
What leaf did not go silver
in the last light?
What hand did not turn us aside?

NOTES

"The Fall of Da Nang"   The title refers to the capture of Da Nang by Viet Cong
and North Vietnamese forces in March 1975. During the final evacuation of the city,
South Vietnamese government soldiers commandeered at gunpoint many of the
planes and boats being used in the evacuation, forcing civilians to stay behind.

"The Hooded Legion"   The title is suggested by the Egyptian god "Ra," the beaked
or hooded figure; also by Robert E. Morrison's novel, *The Bird of Fire*, New York,
Vantage Press, 1978; and by the field jackets issued to American soldiers during the
Vietnam War.

WALTER McDONALD

Walter McDonald was born in 1934 in Lubbock, Texas. A pilot in the United States Air Force, 1957-71, he served briefly in a ground assignment in Vietnam, 1969-70. He holds a B.A. and M.A. from Texas Technological College, and a Ph.D. from the University of Iowa. He is the recipient of a National Endowment for the Arts Fellowship, the Juniper Prize, the George Elliston Poetry Prize, and three Poetry Prizes from the Texas Institute of Letters. He is currently Director of Creative Writing and Paul Whitfield Horn Professor of English at Texas Tech University.

McDonald's poetry has appeared in *Poetry*, *The Atlantic*, *The Kenyon Review*, *American Poetry Review*, *The Antioch Review*, *TriQuarterly*, and *College English*. McDonald has thirteen published books, including eleven volumes of poetry. In addition, he has a forthcoming cycle of short stories about the end of the Vietnam War.

POETRY

Caliban in Blue. Lubbock: Texas Tech University Press, 1976.
One Thing Leads to Another. New Braunfels, Tex.: Cedar Rock Press, 1978.
Anything, Anything. Seattle, Wash.: L'Epervier Press, 1980.
Burning the Fence. Lubbock: Texas Tech University Press, 1981.
Working Against Time. Walnut Creek, Calif.: Calliope Press, 1981.
Witching on Hardscrabble. Peoria, Ill.: Spoon River Poetry Press, 1985.
The Flying Dutchman. Columbus, Ohio: Ohio State University Press, 1987.
After the Noise of Saigon. Amherst: University of Massachusetts Press, 1988.
Splitting Wood for Winter. Denton: University of North Texas Press, 1988.
Rafting the Brazos. Denton: University of North Texas Press, 1988.
Night Landings. New York: Harper & Row. Forthcoming.

FICTION

A Band of Brothers. Lubbock: Texas Tech University Press. Forthcoming.

EDITED WORKS

With Frederick Kiley, *A 'Catch-22' Casebook.* New York: Thomas Y. Crowell Company, Inc., 1973.
With James P. White. *Texas Stories & Poems.* Dallas: Texas Center for Writers Press, 1978.

The Winter before the War

In fall we raked
the leaves downhill
in heaps high
as the fence,
set them afire
and watched them
burn. In hours
the fire died down,

the mounds of leaves
only a smudge
of black.

Weeks later
the first snow fell.
Weeks after that
the lake one hundred
yards away was solid,
white, the ice so thick
trucks drove on it.
Fishermen wrapped up like bears
chopped through the ice,
let down their hooks
and waited. Their breaths
resembled chimney smoke.
We pulled the sled
across the lake,
our children
bundled up
and eating snow.
The fireplace
after dark
was where we thawed.
Chocolate steamed
in mugs we wrapped
our hands around.
Our children slept.
The news came on.
We watched
each other's eyes.

For Kelly,
Missing in Action

When you disappeared
over the North
I pulled down *Dubliners*.

What strange counterparts,
you and the Cong.

You, who said no one would make
General
reading Joyce,
named your F-4 "The Dead,"
and dropped out of the sun
like some death angel
playing mumbledy peg
with bombs.

I never knew what launched
the search for Araby in you,
that wholly secular search
for thrills.

I wonder how you felt
when they strapped on the bombs
that first flight North.
Did it seem at all like
bearing a chalice through a throng of
foes, or finally,
as you let them go
did you see yourself in the plexiglass
a creature masked
derided by vanity
dead as Dublin,
far from home?

Faraway Places

This daughter watching ducks knows
nothing of Vietnam,
this pond her only Pacific,
separation to her
only the gulf between herself
and ducks that others feed.
"They will come," he calms her, "soon,"
and touches her. Her hair blows
golden in the wind. Strange prospect
to leave such gold, he thinks.

There is no gold for him
in Asia.

The ducks parade unsatisfied,
now gliding to her hand, her bread,
her tenderness. Possession
turns on him like swimming ducks,
forcing his touch again.

She does not feel his claim
upon her gold
that swirls upon her face but cannot blink
her eyes
so full of ducks.

War Games

Crouched in a sandbagged bunker,
lights out, listening for rockets,
we played the game with nothing
in our hands, pretending dice

clicked in our fists and hit the dirt floor
rolling. Snake eyes, boxcars,
the point to make, someone
calling our luck, no one

we could see, all of us in this
together. Rockets that crashed down
on the base always killed somebody else.
We played with nothing to lose,

the crews on night shift
risking no more than us,
no sand bunker safe from a hit.
We rolled till our luck ran out,

passed the empty handful
to the next man kneeling
in the dark, bunkered down,
having the time of our lives.

We never knew the color of scrip
we lost, not caring
what was at stake in night games,
not daring to think.

When the all-clear siren wailed
we lifted our winnings from dust
and left through the reeking tunnel
into moonlight naked as day

and climbed the steps of our barracks
to wire springs tight as our nerves,
lying in rooms flashing red
from flames in the distance.

Caliban in Blue

Off again,
thrusting up at scald
of copper in orient west
I climb into such blue skies.
Skies even here
belong to Setobos:
calls it air power.
Air power is peace power,
his motto catechizes
as we, diving, spout
flame from under,
off in one hell
of a roar.

His arms like radar
point the spot.
For this, I trained to salivate
and tingle, target-diving,
hand enfolding hard throttle
in solitary masculine delight.

Focused on cross hairs,
eyes glazing, hand triggers switches in
pulsing orgasm,

savage release;
pull out
and off we go again
thrusting deep
into the martial lascivious blue
of uncle's sky.

Interview
with a Guy Named Fawkes,
U.S. Army

—you tell them this—
tell them shove it, they're
not here, tell them kiss
my rear when they piss about
women and kids in shacks
we fire on. damn.
they fire on us.
hell yes, it's war
they sent us for.
what do they know back where
not even in their granddam's days
did any damn red rockets glare.
don't tell me
how chips fall.
those are The Enemy:
waste them all.

Rocket Attack

(AP)—Enemy gunners lobbed seven Russian-made
100 lb. rockets into the American base at Cam Ranh
Bay last night. Damage was reported light. Four
Americans were wounded, and three Vietnamese
civilians were killed.

Rocks fallout on us
like mountains,
crash of those impacting
richer than thunder,

concussion sharp as wood on wood
slamming shut my coffin.

Another on its way
maybe

seconds

like lightning
within
bursting,
smashing everything.

Little mouths
little hands I saw
in the Vietnamese airmen's
shacks—
little laughter
clipped, shrill, grating
on my western nerves.
Daughter, oh God, my daughter
may she never
safe at home
Never hear the horrible
sucking sound a rocket makes when it

.

For Harper,
Killed in Action

When they brought you down
over the Plain of Jars
I thought of when you
volunteered for photo runs
from Udorn into Laos.
Better to take pictures
than to bomb, you said.
I do not blame. My taxes
paid your fares.

I hope it was a lucky shot,
sudden,

not some gunner blinded to your loss
cheering as your solid
flesh impacted
in the common ground.

The Retired Pilot
to Himself

I come to the simplest things
last. Even flying
I was slow,
rehearsing take-offs before sleep,
spinning solo
others merely logged as spun.
Last discovering the fun
meant war—
chandelles and Immelmanns
and Cuban Eights,
ecstatic murder in the skies too strange,
too wonderful to grasp.

Bombs so long falling; after falling,
what release?
          0 for tonight—
my child
with benediction
sidling heel and toe in graceful
rhapsody,
acceptance of herself.

Once You've Been to War

There are times when everything I touch
turns to leaves, my plot of earth breathing
like women who seem to be always fertile,
their nurseries teeming with mouths,
flower-print dresses forever bulging.

Whatever I plant at night in dreams
by dawn has rooted, ferns like veils,

orchids, fuchsia tendrils reaching for trees,
my secret back yard dense as the front,
three canopies of rain forest

chittering with spider monkeys,
toucans, orange and black minahs,
birds of paradise. And there are times
deep in my pillow below three canopies
of rain forest I did not plant

but helped to burn, the sandbags burst
and sand blows over everything.
Concertina wire can't hold it back.
Roaches blue-bronzed and emerald,
the size of condors,

tweezer their way over dunes
the winds shuffle and fold like cards.
Rockets slam down beyond the trees,
fallout clatters the leaves
like hail. In parched riverbeds

fish keep flopping,
jets diving are lightning without rain,
and in the distance, bombs explode so long
the hollows of my knees flutter
like flutes whittled from bone.

New Guy

I saw girls squatting against the wall,
and backed out, surely the men's shower,
and it was, the sign said it was mine,
my first day under mortars and rockets

at Tan Son Nhut. Only men lived
in those barracks. Resigned, I entered
the wide corridor of open showers.
They never glanced at me, three girls

and a wrinkled woman. This was their
stall, after so many rooms to scrub,
mops propped in buckets before them
like bamboo stakes. They seemed camped

for the day, with Asian patience.
Two other men scrubbed themselves naked
in suds, and ignored them. With miles of maps
to go over before I slept, facing the wall,

I stripped, shivered and soaped in the cold
water of Saigon, my eyes closed,
listening underwater to alien voices
like angels speaking in tongues.

The Food Pickers of Saigon

Rubbish like compost heaps burned every hour
of my days and nights at Tan Son Nhut.
Ragpickers scoured the edges of our junk,
risking the flames, bent over,
searching for food. A ton of tin cans

piled up each month, sharp edged, unlabeled.
Those tiny anonymous people could stick
their hands inside and claw out whatever
remained, scooping it into jars, into their
mouths. No one went hungry. At a distance,

the dump was like a coal mine fire burning
out of control, or Moses' holy bush
which was not consumed. Watching them labor
in the field north of my barracks, trying
to think of something good to write my wife,

I often thought of bears in Yellowstone
our first good summer in a tent. I wrote
about the bears, helping us both focus
on how they waddled to the road and begged,
and came some nights into the campground

so long ago and took all food they found.
We sat helplessly naive outside our tent
and watched them, and one night rolled
inside laughing when one great bear
turned and shoulder-swayed his way toward us.

Through the zipped mosquito netting
we watched him watching us. Slack-jawed,
he seemed to grin, to thank us for all
he was about to receive from our table.
We thought how lovely, how much fun

to be this close to danger. No campers
had died in that Disneyland national park
for years. Now, when my children
eat their meat and bread and leave
good broccoli or green beans

on their plates, I call them back
and growl, I can't help it. It's like hearing
my father's voice again. I never tell them
why they have to eat it. I never say
they're like two beautiful children

I found staring at me one night
through the screen of my window,
at Tan Son Nhut, bone-faced. Or that
when I crawled out of my stifling monsoon
dream to feed them, they were gone.

Christmas Bells, Saigon

Buses came late, each driver sullen,
head shaved above the ears. At the French
country club on base we nursed warm drinks
while French and their Viet Cong cousins
ignored us, strolling from room to room.

The maître d' said wait, he'd find a place
for us. For hours, we stumbled around outside
trying to get drunk. After weeks of rockets

we needed to celebrate. Someone joked
the clerk who took our reservation

died in last night's rockets. People I knew
kept disappearing. I asked what's going on.
Vietnamese friends all looked at me
and shrugged. Men who'd been in Vietnam
for years kept dancing off with girls.

I listened for gunfire above the band's
loud brassy mix of Beatles and Japanese.
I studied guards buried in cages
ten feet above us in trees. Five minutes apart
they rattled bells to signal—what?—

We are alive? How could anyone believe
in bells dangled on barbed wires?
Sappers smart enough to count
could slit the guards and keep it up,
ring-ring, till all guard stations fell.

Two sergeants and I sat on a verandah
and wondered where all the girls had gone,
when a bus to the barracks would come,
blamed bad French planters for the war.
Even with rockets, I wanted to lie down

and dream of peace, rumors of good will
toward men. We agreed on all things true
and noble, sober on gin and French vermouth,
listening to Japanese Beatles and the bells,
the bells all through the night.

After the Noise of Saigon

If where we hunt defines us,
then stalking this steep hillside
dark with spruce makes sense,

more than the dreams I've floundered in
for years, trying to fathom signs
all night and wading ashore

disgusted. Switches dripping sap
keep flipping me when I glance
over my shoulder for spoor

I might have missed. Evergreen
needles sting when I swing my head
face-forward for clues. Isn't this

the strangest nightmare of all,
knowing my aim with a bow
is no better at twenty yards

than forty? But here I am, alone
with a cougar I've stalked for hours,
climbing until I'm dizzy.

These blue trees have nothing
and all to do with what I'm here for
after the noise of Saigon,

the simple bitter sap that rises in me
like bad blood I need to spill
out here alone in the silence

of deep woods, far from people I know
who see me as a friend, not some damned
madman stumbling for his life.

For Friends Missing in Action

Into this tunnel of dirt
deposit quick thoughts
of a corpse
like savings. Pitiful beer

can't dig him up
from seventy shovels of earth,

but toast him over and over.
Here lies a flier

missing since Saigon
fell in the seventies,
sixes or sevens
if he cratered deep in a swamp,

brought down in flames
from twenty thousand feet
by a rocket, or languished,
chained to a bamboo cesspool.

He's gone.
Lift up your savage mugs
and let the truth ring
like a gong: he's gone.

NOTES

"**Caliban in Blue**" Caliban is the savage and deformed slave in William Shakespeare's play, *The Tempest*. Setobos is an allusion to Robert Browning's poem "Caliban Upon Setobos." Uncle refers to Caliban's version of "Uncle Sam" or the United States government.

"**Interview with a Guy Named Fawkes, U.S. Army**" The title is a play on Guy Fawkes, a seventeenth-century English radical who attempted to blow up Parliament.

"**The Food Pickers of Saigon**" Moses' holy bush is a reference to the burning bush in the Old Testament book of Exodus, Chapter 3, from which God spoke to Moses.

BASIL T. PAQUET

Basil T. Paquet was born in 1944 in Hartford, Connecticut. He was drafted into the United States Army as a conscientious objector and served, 1966-68, as a medic, including service in Vietnam, 1967-68 with the Twenty-fourth Evacuation Hospital. Winner of the Wallace Stevens Award for Poetry, he holds a B.A. and an M.A. from the University of Connecticut. He is currently a management consultant.

Paquet's poems have appeared in *The New York Review of Books*, *Freedomways*, *Midwest Magazine*, *WIN Magazine*, *New Times*, *Long Island Review*, and *Jamaica Arts Review* and have been anthologized in *Vietnam Anthology*. In addition, Paquet is the co-editor of two anthologies:

With Jan Barry and Larry Rottmann. *Winning Hearts and Minds: War Poems by Vietnam Veterans*. Brooklyn, N.Y.: 1st Casualty Press, 1972; New York: McGraw-Hill, 1972.

With Wayne Karlin and Larry Rottmann. *Free Fire Zone: Short Stories by Vietnam Veterans*. Coventry, Conn.: 1st Casualty Press; New York: McGraw-Hill, 1973.

They Do Not Go Gentle

The half-dead comatose
Paw the air like cats do when they dream.
They perform isometrics tirelessly.
They flail the air with a vengeance
You know they cannot have.
After all, their multiplication tables,
Memories of momma, and half their id
Lies in some shell hole
Or plop! splatter! on your jungle boots.
It must be some atavistic angst
Of their muscle and bones,
Some ancient ritual of their sea water self,
Some blood stream monsoon,
Some sinew storm that makes
Their bodies rage on tastelessly
Without their shattered brains.

In a Plantation

The bullet passed
Through his right temple,
His left side
Could not hold

Against the metal,
His last "I am" exploded
Red and grey on a rubber tree.

Night Dust-off

A sound like hundreds of barbers
stropping furiously, increases;
suddenly the night lights,
flashing blades thin bodies
into red strips
hunched against the wind
of a settling slickship.

Litters clatter open,
hands reaching
into the dark belly of the ship
touch toward moans,
they are thrust into a privy,
feeling into wounds,
the dark belly all wound,
all wet screams riven limbs
moving in the beaten night.

Basket Case

I waited eighteen years to become a man.
My first woman was a whore off Tu Do street,
But I wish I never felt the first wild
Gliding lust, because the rage and thrust
Of a mine caught me hip high.
I felt the rip at the walls of my thighs,
A thousand metal scythes cut me open,
My little fish shot twenty yards
Into a swamp canal.
I fathered only this—the genderless bitterness
Of two stumps, and an unwanted pity
That births the faces of all
Who will see me till I die deliriously
From the spreading sepsis that was once my balls.

Morning—A Death

Turn—Character 1

I've blown up your chest for thirty minutes
And crushed it down an equal time,
And still you won't warm to my kisses.
I've sucked and puffed on your
Metal No. 8 throat for so long,
And twice you've moaned under my thrusts
On your breastbone. I've worn off
Those sparse hairs you counted noble on your chest,
And twice you defibrillated,
And twice blew back my breath.
I've scanned the rhythms of your living,
Forced half-rhymes in your silent pulse,
Sprung brief spondees in your lungs,
And the caesura's called mid-line, half-time,
Incomplete, but with a certain finality.
The bullet barks apocalyptic
And you don't unzip your sepulchral
Canvas bag in three days.
No rearticulation of nucleics, no phoenix,
No novae, just an arbitrary of one-way bangs
Flowing out to interstitial calms.
The required canonical wait for demotion
To lower order, and you wash out pure chemical.
You are dead just as finally
As your mucosity dries on my lips
In this morning sun.
I have thumped and blown into your kind too often,
I grow tired of kissing the dead.

Counterturn—Character 2

I'd sooner be a fallen pine cone this winter
In a cradle of cold New England rock,
Less hurt in it than nineteen years.
What an exit! Stage left, fronds waving,
Cut down running my ass off at a tree line.
I'm thinking, as I hear my chest
Sucking air through its brand new nipple,

113

I bought the ticket, I hope I drown fast,
The pain is all in living.

Stand—Character 1

I grow so tired of jostled litters
Filling the racks, and taking off
Your tags and rings, pulling out
Your metal throats and washing
Your spittle down with warm beer at night,
So tired of tucking you all in,
And smelling you all on me for hours.
I'd sooner be in New England this winter
With pine pitch on my hands than your blood,
Lightly fondling breasts and kissing
Women's warm mouths than thumping
Your shattered chests and huffing
In your broken lips or aluminum windpipes,
Sooner lift a straying hair from her wet mouth
Than a tear of elephant grass from your slack lips.
I'd so much rather be making children,
Than tucking so many in.

Easter '68

I have seen the paschal men today.
Long past rising to a passion
they sucked their last sun
through blued lips,
buttressed their intestines in handfuls,
lifting their wounds to the sky
they fell silent as the sun,
as words not spoken,
broken Easters of flesh
girdled in fatigue strips,
red arching rainbows of dead men
rising like a promise
to give Jesus the big kiss
and sinking down—
only my breath on their lips,
only my words on their mouths.

It Is Monsoon at Last

The black peak at Xuan Loc
pulls a red apron of light
up from the east.
105s and 155s are walking shells
toward us from Bear Cat
down some trail
washing a trail in fire.

An eagle flight snakes west toward Lai Khe,
a demonstration of lights
flashing green and red across a sky still black above.
Our boots rattle off the boardwalk
Cha-Chat-Cha-Chat
the sound spills across the helipad
out towards the forest
out towards the dawn;
it chases devil dusters
out to the jungle.

The boardwalk bends
with our ungainly walk
litter handles creak
with the heavy weight of the dead,
the dull whoosh and thud of B-40s
sounds south along the berm
the quick flat answer of 16s follows.

Gunships are going up
sucking devil dusters into the air.
We can see them through the morgue door
against the red froth clouds
hanging over Xuan Loc.
We lift the boy into a death bag.
We lift the boy into the racks.
We are building a bunker of dead.
We are stacking the dead for protection.

This dead boy is on my hands
My thighs are wet with the vomit of death

His blood is on my mouth
My mouth My mouth tastes his blood.

The gunships are firing over the Dong Nai
throwing fire into the river
clouds are coming in from the sea
I can smell the rain, see it
over Xuan Loc, over me
it is monsoon at last.

Graves Registration

From the trucks we see
the black shark fin of Xuan Loc
break from the swelling green sea jungle,
cutting the thick red air of dusk.
The sound of the engines washes
into the gullies of heaped wire
strung with bodies spilling toward the village
like a trail of crushed sea forms.
Great fish-mountain
did you show your grin here?
Did your face break surface,
mouth of magnificent death?
The tank shells are like popped cans,
their meat turning in the sun.
Carapace, claws, antennae—
debris all stiff with death
and swelled by the panting sun,
what are we to do with you?

"Too many. We'll get another truck."

"Fuck the gooks. We'll use lime."

"Kipper, stay with the bodies!"

The land cannot hold you all,
it is filling with debris.
We will have to ship some home
for recycling.
When the truck comes back

we will wrap you in plastic—zip! zip!
You brown-yellow guys
are going to get some whiteness,
you're going home to Xuan Loc "passing."
Rotting into the earth in dusted rows,
seeping into the earth in chemicals,
your moisture already lifting into the air
to rub the dark fin in night mists,
to cover us with your breath
while we lie drunken in our camps.

This morning you all
must have been violent!
Strung out along this road
like tatters on the wire
you seem a strange attack.
I heard your noise in the early darkness
from my hootch,
I toasted your anarchy with gin.
Did you all think death?
Did you speak in whispers
or shout at war
in quick metal breath?
Did you shout at death,
or did he glide into your mouths
while you sucked some J's?

"The brightness of sun
caught this morning
in his red fist
the smashed flowers
of our faces,
licked the wetness
the drying surprise   "Something crushed my
from our petal-eyes   face. I was thinking of
and reeled on."   freedom and hunger."

"I used to salty dog
and tongue with laughter
soft brown breast heads."

"The sky trod us in walking shells,
our eyes shallow pools

117

        for the tongues of flies
        and a thirsty sun."
"I remember a cloud
against the flares.
I was high as a mother.   "We are the ripped forest,
It looked like a fish."   men who became the jungle,
                         limed limbs whitening,
                         silent as the mountain,
                         as the last seal of lips."

"Laughter shredded in my mouth.
I felt my throat rip in a choke,
the earth heaved with flame."
           "Tonight the paleness of moon will
           light on our stilled limbs,
           flutter with clouds,
           and fly to deeper night
           with carrion of our dreams."

        "The beast moved among us,
        our voices hurled back
        by the fire,
        we fell silent, unhurried
        as the whorl
        on stiff red fingertips."

Why do I move among you
like a berserk ballerina,
tippy-toeing over you
filling out your tags
and powdering the rest?
I cannot believe anymore
that names count.
I fear some day
the beast will come for me,
but that we will rush
to each other like lovers,
secret sharers in the memory of your passing.
Even more I fear that

some day
I will be the only one remembering.

I wish you could share this
joint with me.

The trucks will be back soon.

Mourning the Death, by Hemorrhage, of a Child from Honai

Always the children are included
In these battles for the body politic.
Prefaced with mortars and rockets
The Year of the Monkey was preluded
By the mephitic
Stench of blasted bodies sullenly drifting from the pocket

Of refugee hootches at Honai.
The enemy patriots knew the young
Would be glad to die for the revolution.
The allies were certain the vox populi
Called a mandate for flag-strung
Counterattack and awful retribution.

The majesty of the annihilation of the city
Could be heard clearly in the background,
I could only wonder what ideology
The child carried in her left arm—necessity
Must have dictated an M-16 round
Should cut it off, and her gaining the roll of martyrology.

Her dying in my arms, this daughter
Weaned on war, was for the greater
Glory of all concerned.
There was no time to mourn your slaughter
Small, denuded, one-armed thing, I too was violator,
And after the first death, the many must go unmourned.

Group Shot

So they passed,
Days of hollow cadence
When each passing day
Seemed an album of daguerreotypes,
Camera-caught, anachronistic.
Puffed-up, pigeon-breasted,
As in Brady's day
We strutted to a distant
Very insistent drum.

I have photos of us all together,
Polished boots and brass
In front of whitewashed barracks.
There, hanging on the parlor wall,
We are as once we were,
The wholeness of our limbs,
Two eyes blinking at the sun,
When all had all needed
To woo the world.

NOTES

"Graves Registration" Kipper's bitterly ironical reference to "passing" refers to the ability of a person of one racial type to pass himself or herself off as another racial type. The term is most commonly encountered in the United States in reference to the long period of racial segregation following the Civil War, when light-skinned Negroes were sometimes able to pass themselves off in public as Caucasians, thus avoiding the restrictions created by racial discrimination.

"Mourning the Death, by Hemorrhage, of a Child from Honai" The title is a play on the Dylan Thomas poem, "A Refusal to Mourn the Death, by Fire, of a Child in London."

According to the author, the village of Honai in South Vietnam was known as Sniper's Village; after the Tet Offensive of 1968, it became known as "Widow's Village."

The Year of the Monkey refers to 1968 and the Tet Offensive.

BRUCE WEIGL

Bruce Weigl was born in 1949 in Lorain, Ohio. He served in the United States Army, 1967-70, including service in Vietnam, 1967-68. He holds a B.A. from Oberlin College, an M.A. from the University of New Hampshire, and a Ph.D. from the University of Utah. He is the recipient of a Pushcart Prize, an Academy of American Poets Prize, a Breadloaf Fellowship in Poetry, a YADDO Foundation Fellowship, and a National Endowment for the Arts Fellowship. Currently, he is associate professor of English at Pennsylvania State University.

Weigl's poetry has appeared in *American Poetry Review, Paris Review, Mother Jones, TriQuarterly, Western Humanities Review, Prairie Schooner, Field*, and *Harpers*, and has been anthologized in *Unwinding the Vietnam War* and *The Morrow Anthology of Younger American Poets*. Weigl has seven published books:

POETRY

A Sackful of Old Quarrels. Cleveland, Ohio: Cleveland State University Poetry Center, 1976.

Executioner. Tucson, Ariz.: Ironwood Press, 1977.

A Romance. Pittsburgh, Pa.: University of Pittsburgh Press, 1979.

The Monkey Wars. Athens, Ga.: University of Georgia Press, 1984.

Song of Napalm. New York: Atlantic Monthly Press, 1988.

EDITED WORKS

The Giver of Morning: On the Poetry of Dave Smith. Birmingham, Ala.: Thunder Mountain Press, 1982.

With T. R. Hummer. *The Imagination as Glory: On the Poetry of James Dickey*. Champaign: University of Illinois Press, 1985.

Sailing to Bien Hoa

In my dream of the hydroplane
I'm sailing to Bien Hoa
the shrapnel in my thighs
like tiny glaciers.
I remember a flower,
a kite, a mannikin playing the guitar,
a yellow fish eating a bird, a truck
floating in urine, a rat carrying a banjo,
a fool counting the cards, a monkey praying,
a procession of whales, and far off
two children eating rice,
speaking French—
I'm sure of the children,
their damp flutes,
the long line of their vowels.

Surrounding Blues on the Way Down

I was barely in country. December, hot,
we slipped under rain black clouds
opening around us like orchids.
He'd come to take me into the jungle
so I felt the loneliness
though I did not yet hate the beautiful war.
Eighteen years old and a man
was telling me how to stay alive
in the tropics he said would rot me—

Brothers of the heart he said and smiled
until we came upon a mama san
bent over from her stuffed sack of flowers.
We flew past her
but he hit the brakes hard,
he spun the tires backwards in the mud.
He did not hate the war either
but other reasons made him cry out to her
so she stopped,
she smiled her beetle black teeth at us,
she raised her arms in the air.

I have no excuse for myself,
I sat in that man's jeep in the rain
and watched him slam her to her knees,
the plastic butt of his M-16
crashing down on her.
I was barely in country, the clouds
hung like huge flowers, black
like her teeth.

Girl at the Chu Lai Laundry

All this time I had forgotten.
My miserable platoon was moving out
one day in the war and I had my clothes in the laundry.
I ran the two dirt miles.
Convoy already forming behind me. I hit
the block of small hooches and saw her

twist out the black rope of her hair in the sun.
She did not look up at me,
not even when I called to her for my clothes.
She said I couldn't have them,
they were wet. . . .

Who would've thought the world stops
turning in the war, the tropical heat like hate
and your platoon moves out without you,
your wet clothes piled
at the feet of the girl at the laundry,
beautiful with her facts.

Mines

1

In Vietnam I was always afraid of mines:
North Vietnamese mines, Vietcong mines,
French mines, American mines,
whole fields marked with warning signs.

A Bouncing Betty comes up waist high,
cuts you in half.
One man's legs were laid
alongside him in the Dustoff,
he asked for a chairback, morphine,
he screamed he wanted to give
his eyes away, his kidneys,
his heart . . .

2

Here is how you walk at night: slowly lift
one leg, clear the sides with your arms, clear the back,
front, put the leg down, like swimming.

Temple Near Quang Tri, Not on the Map

Dusk, the ivy thick with sparrows
squawking for more room
is all we hear; we see

birds move on the walls of the temple
shaping their calligraphy of wings.
Ivy is thick in the grottoes,
on the moon-watching platform
and ivy keeps the door from fully closing.

The point man leads us and we are
inside, lifting
the white wash bowl, the smaller bowl
for rice, the stone lanterns
and carved stone heads that open
above the carved faces for incense.
But even the bamboo sleeping mat
rolled in the corner,
even the place of prayer is clean.
And a small man

sits legs askew in the shadow
the farthest wall casts
halfway across the room.
He is bent over, his head
rests on the floor, and he is speaking something
as though to us and not to us.
The CO wants to ignore him;
he locks and loads and fires a clip into the walls
which are not packed with rice this time
and tells us to move out.

But one of us moves towards the man,
curious about what he is saying.
We bend him to sit straight up
and when he is nearly peaked
at the top of his slow uncurling
his face becomes visible, his eyes
roll down to the charge
wired between his chin and the floor.
The sparrows
burst off the walls into the jungle.

The Sharing

I have not ridden a horse much,
two, maybe three times,
a broken gray mare my cousin called Ghost.
Then only in the Fall
through the flat pastures of Ohio.
That's not much,
but I watched two Chinese tanks
roll out of the jungle side by side,
their turret guns feeling before them
like a man walking through his dream,
their tracks slapping the bamboo like hooves.

I can't name the gaits of a horse
except the canter,
and that rocks you high to the withers,
but I saw those arms,
those guns and did not know for a moment
what they were, but knew they were not horses
as they pulled themselves deep
into the triple-canopy jungle
until there was only the dull rattle of their tracks
and a boy on a gray horse,
flying through the opening fields.

Burning Shit at An Khe

Into that pit
    I had to climb down
with a rake and matches; eventually,
    you had to do something
because it just kept piling up
    and it wasn't our country, it wasn't
our air thick with the sick smoke
    so another soldier and I
lifted the shelter off its blocks
    to expose the homemade toilets:
fifty-five gallon drums cut in half
    with crude wood seats that splintered.

We soaked the piles in fuel oil
    and lit the stuff
and tried to keep the fire burning.
    To take my first turn
I paid some kid
    a care package of booze from home.
I'd walked past the burning once
    and gagged the whole heart of myself,
it smelled like the world
    was on fire,
but when my turn came again
    there was no one
so I stuffed cotton up my nose
    and marched up that hill. We poured
and poured until it burned and black
    smoke curdled
but the fire went out.
    Heavy artillery
hammered the evening away in the distance,
    Vietnamese laundry women watched
from a safe place, laughing.
    I'd grunted out eight months
of jungle and thought I had a grip on things
    but we flipped the coin and I lost
and climbed down into my fellow soldiers'
    shit and began to sink and didn't stop
until I was deep to my knees. Liftships
    cut the air above me, the hacking
blast of their blades
    ripped dust in swirls so every time
I tried to light a match
    it died
and it all came down on me, the stink
    and the heat and the worthlessness
until I slipped and climbed
    out of that hole and ran
past the olive drab
    tents and trucks and clothes and everything
green as far from the shit
    as the fading light allowed.
Only now I can't fly.
    I lie down in it

and finger paint the words of who I am
    across my chest
until I'm covered and there's only one smell,
    one word.

Song for the Lost Private

The night we were to meet in the hotel
in the forbidden Cholon district
you didn't show
so I drank myself into a filthy
room with a bar girl
who had terrible scars
she ran her fingers over
as we bartered for the night.
But drunk I couldn't do anything, angry
I threw the mattress to the street
and stood out on the balcony naked,
cursing your name to the night.
She thought I was crazy and tried to give my money back.
I don't know how to say I tried again,
I saw myself in the mirror and couldn't move.
She crushed the paper money in her fist
and curled in sleep away from me
so I felt cruel, cold, and small arms fire
cracked in the marketplace below.
I thought I heard you call back my name
but white flares lit the sky
casting the empty streets in clean light
and the firing stopped.
I couldn't sleep so I touched her
small shoulders, traced the curve of her spine,
traced the scars,
the miles we were all from home.

Him, on the Bicycle

There was no light; there was no light at all . . .
—ROETHKE

In a liftship near Hue
the door gunner is in a trance.
He's that driver who falls
asleep at the wheel
between Pittsburgh and Cleveland
staring at the Ho Chi Minh trail.

Flares fall,
where the river leaps
I go stiff,
I have to think, tropical.

The door gunner sees movement;
the pilot makes small circles:
four men running, carrying rifles,
one man on a bicycle.

He pulls me out of the ship;
there's firing far away.
I'm on the back of the bike
holding his hips.
It's hard pumping for two.
I hop off and push the bike.

I'm brushing past trees,
the man on the bike stops pumping,
lifts his feet,
we don't waste a stroke.
His hat flies off,
I catch it behind my back,
put it on, I want to live forever!

Like a blaze
streaming down the trail.

Anna Grasa

I came home from Vietnam.
My father had a sign
made at the foundry.
WELCOME HOME BRUCE
in orange glow paint.
He rented spotlights,
I had to squint.
WELCOME HOME BRUCE.

Out of the car I moved
up on the sign
dreaming myself full,
the sign that cut the sky,
my eyes burned.

But behind the terrible thing
I saw my grandmother,
beautiful Anna Grasa.
I couldn't tell her, tell her.

I clapped to myself,
clapped to the sound of her dress.
I could have put it on
she held me so close,
both of us could be inside.

Monkey

Out of the horror there rises a musical ache that is
beautiful . . .
— JAMES WRIGHT

1
I am you are he she it is
they are you are we are.
I am you are he she it is
they are you are we are.
When they ask for your number
pretend to be breathing.

129

Forget the stinking jungle,
force your fingers between the lines.
Learn to get out of the dew.
The snakes are thirsty.
Bladders, water, boil it, drink it.
Get out of your clothes:
you can't move in your green clothes.
Your O.D. in color issue.
Get out the plates and those who ate,
those who spent the night.
Those small Vietnamese soldiers.
They love to hold your hand.
Back away from their dark cheeks.
Small Vietnamese soldiers.
They love to love you.
I have no idea how it happened,
I remember nothing but light.

2

I don't remember the hard
swallow of the lover.
I don't remember the burial of ears.
I don't remember
the time of the explosion.
This is the place curses are manufactured:
delivered like white tablets.
The survivor is spilling his bedpan.
He slips a curse into your pocket,
you're finally satisfied.
I don't remember the heat
in the hands,
the heat around the neck.

Good times bad times sleep
get up work. Sleep get up
good times bad times.
Work eat sleep good bad work times.
I like a certain cartoon of wounds.
The water which refused to dry.
I like a little unaccustomed mercy.
Pulling the trigger is all we have.
I hear a child.

3

I dropped to the bottom of a well.
I have a knife.
I cut someone with it.
Oh, I have the petrified eyebrows
of my Vietnam monkey.
My monkey from Vietnam.
My monkey.
Put your hand here.
It makes no sense.
I beat the monkey.
I didn't know him.
He was bloody.
He lowered his intestines
to my shoes. My shoes
spit-shined the moment
I learned to tie the bow.
I'm not on speaking terms
with anyone. In the wrong climate
a person can spoil,
the way a pair of boots slows you down. . . .

I don't know when I'm sleeping.
I don't know if what I'm saying
is anything at all.
I'll lie on my monkey bones.

4

I'm tired of the rice
falling in slow motion
like eggs from the smallest animal.
I'm twenty-five years old,
quiet, tired of the same mistakes,
the same greed, the same past.
The same past with its bleat
and pound of the dead,
with its hand grenade
tossed into a hootch on a dull Sunday
because when a man dies like that
his eyes sparkle,
his nose fills with witless nuance
because a farmer in Bong Son

has dead cows lolling
in a field of claymores
because the VC tie hooks to their comrades
because a spot of blood
is a number
because a woman is lifting
her dress across the big pond.

If we're soldiers we should smoke them
if we have them. Someone's bound
to point us in the right direction
sooner or later.

I'm tired and I'm glad you asked.

5
There is a hill.
Men run top hill.
Men take hill.
Give hill to man.

Me and my monkey
and me and my monkey
my Vietnamese monkey
my little brown monkey
came with me
to Guam and Hawaii
in Ohio he saw
my people he
jumped on my daddy
he slipped into mother
he baptized my sister
he's my little brown monkey
he came here from heaven
to give me his spirit imagine
my monkey my beautiful
monkey he saved me lifted
me above the punji
sticks above the mines
above the ground burning
above the dead above
the living above the

wounded dying the wounded
dying.

Men take hill away from smaller men.
Men take hill and give to fatter man.
Men take hill. Hill has number.
Men run up hill. Run down.

On The Anniversary of Her Grace

Rain and low clouds blown through the valley,
rain down the coast raising the brackish
rivers at their high tides too high,
rain and black skies that come for you.

I wake from a restless night of dreams of her
whom I will never have again
as surely as each minute passing
makes impossible another small fulfillment
until there's only a lingering
I remember, a kiss I had imagined
would come again and again to my face.

Inside me the war had eaten a hole.
I could not touch anyone.
The wind blew through me to the green place
where they still fell in their blood.
I could hear their voices at night.
I could not undress in the light
her body cast in the dark rented room.

I could keep the dragons at the gate.
I could paint my face and hide
as shadow in the triple-canopy jungle.
I could not eat or sleep then walk all day
and all night watch a moonlit path for movement.

I could draw leeches from my skin
with the tip of a lit cigarette
and dig a hole deep enough to save me

before the sun bloodied the hills we could not take
even with our lives
but I could not open my arms to her
that first night of forgiveness.
I could not touch anyone.
I thought my body would catch fire.

Song of Napalm

for my wife

After the storm, after the rain stopped pounding,
we stood in the doorway watching horses
walk off lazily across the pasture's hill.
We stared through the black screen,
our vision altered by the distance
so I thought I saw a mist
kicked up around their hooves when they faded
like cut-out horses
away from us.
The grass was never more blue in that light, more
scarlet; beyond the pasture
trees scraped their voices into the wind, branches
crisscrossed the sky like barbed wire
but you said they were only branches.

Okay. The storm stopped pounding.
I am trying to say this straight: for once
I was sane enough to pause and breathe
outside my wild plans and after the hard rain
I turned my back on the old curses. I believed
they swung finally away from me . . .

But still the branches are wire
and thunder is the pounding mortar,
still I close my eyes and see the girl
running from her village, napalm
stuck to her dress like jelly,

her hands reaching for the no one
who waits in waves of heat before her.

So I can keep on living,
so I can stay here beside you,
I try to imagine she runs down the road and wings
beat inside her until she rises
above the stinking jungle and her pain
eases, and your pain, and mine.

But the lie swings back again.
The lie works only as long as it takes to speak
and the girl runs only as far
as the napalm allows
until her burning tendons and crackling
muscles draw her up
into that final position
burning bodies so perfectly assume. Nothing
can change that; she is burned behind my eyes
and not your good love and not the rain-swept air
and not the jungle green
pasture unfolding before us can deny it.

Amnesia

If there was a world more disturbing than this
where black clouds bowed down and swallowed you whole
and overgrown tropical plants
rotted, effervescent in the muggy twilight, and monkeys
screamed something
that came to sound like words to each other
across the triple-canopy jungle you shared,
you don't remember it.

You tell yourself no and cry a thousand days.
You imagine that the crows calling autumn into place
are your brothers and you could
if only the strength and will were there
fly up to them to be black
and useful to the wind.

What Saves Us

We are wrapped around each other in
the back of my father's car parked
in the empty lot of the highschool
of our failures, the sweat on her neck
like oil. The next morning I would leave
for the war and I thought I had something
coming for that, I thought to myself
that I would not die never having
been inside her long body. I pulled
her skirt above her waist like an umbrella
blown inside out by the storm. I pulled
her cotton panties up as high as
we could stand. I was on fire. Heaven
was in sight. We were drowning on our
tongues and I tried to tear my pants off
when she stopped so suddenly
we were surrounded by my shuddering
and by the school bells grinding in the
empty halls. She reached to find something,
a silver crucifix on a silver
chain, the tiny savior's head hanging
and stakes through his hands and his feet.
She put it around my neck and held
me so long the black wings of my heart
were calmed . . . We are not always right
about what we think will save us.
I thought that dragging the angel down would
save me, but instead I carried the crucifix
in my pocket and rubbed it on my
face and lips nights the rockets roared in.
People die sometimes so near you
you feel them struggling to cross over.
A deep untangling of one body, from another.

GLOSSARY

(NOTE—Any place name not identified in the glossary, in the notes to the poems, or on the maps is not necessary to understanding the poem in which it appears.)

ammo—ammunition

amtrac—amphibious tractor

ao dai—traditional dress worn by Vietnamese women

ARVN—Army of the Republic of Vietnam (South Vietnam); also, South Vietnamese government soldier

azimuth—term for a line of direction as determined by a compass; used in navigation, artillery fire direction, and air support

Baudelaire—nineteenth century French poet

beaucoup—a lot

beaucoup dien cai dau—roughly translated "very crazy," "insane"

B-40—shoulder-fired anti-tank rocket used by VC/NVA

boonies—boondocks; the field, the hinterlands, the bush (as opposed to more secure rear areas)

BOQ/PX—bachelor officers' quarters and post exchange

Bouncing Betty—type of anti-personnel mine

Brady—Matthew Brady; nineteenth century American photographer, noted especially for his photographs of the Civil War

Buddha grass—type of marijuana

Ca Mau—southern tip of Vietnam

ca loc—type of fish found in Vietnam, similar to a catfish

Captain Gungho—any overly eager officer

C-4—plastic explosive

Central Highlands—area in south Vietnam characterized by mountains and high plateaus, roughly between Saigon and Da Nang but not including coastal regions

Cezanne—nineteenth century French painter

chandelle—type of aerobatic maneuver

Charlie—slang for Viet Cong

Cholon—neighborhood in Saigon populated mainly by ethnic Chinese

chopper—helicopter

claymore—type of antipersonnel mine

CO—meaning depends on context; commanding officer or conscientious objector

Cobra—type of helicopter gunship

concertina wire—coiled barbed wire

Cong—short for Viet Cong
Cong Giao—Catholic
Cowboys—also known as Saigon Cowboys; street punks and illegal draft evaders
crokersack—small burlap bag
Cuban Eight—type of aerobatic maneuver
dau—roughly translated "it hurts"
Delta—Mekong River delta
dink—pejorative slang for Viet Cong or any Asian
Dust-off—helicopter medical evacuation
F4 (F4C)—type of jet fighter-bomber also called a "Phantom"
F-105—United States Air Force jet fighter-bomber
Free Strike Zone—any area officially designated as hostile where United States forces could fire at will and shoot to kill; also known as a free-fire zone
Front—National Front for the Liberation of Vietnam (NLF); political arm of the Viet Cong
Gary Cooper—mid-twentieth-century Hollywood actor
GI—American soldier; literally "government issue"
GI Bill—government-mandated educational benefits for veterans
Ginny—author's high school sweetheart
gook—pejorative slang for Viet Cong or any Vietnamese
grease—slang for kill
Green Beret—United States Army Special Forces; any member of same
Harleys—Harley-Davidson motorcycles
Hendrix—1960s rock musician Jimi Hendrix
Ho Chi Minh Trail—extensive system of trails running from North Vietnam through Laos and Cambodia into South Vietnam
hoa binh—peace
Hoa Ky—United States
Honda 50—type of light motorbike
hootch—house; any structure used as a home or living area
howitzer—field artillery piece
Huey Black Cat—type of helicopter
illumination—parachute flare launched by artillery or aircraft
im—silence
Immelmann—type of aerobatic maneuver
J—joint; marijuana cigarette
Kabuki—highly stylized Japanese drama
kepi—type of cap worn by French Foreign Legionnaires

Klamath Indians—Native American tribe of the Pacific Northwest; remnants of the tribe live on a small reservation in southwestern Oregon near the town of Roseburg and the Umqua River

liftship—helicopter

LT (Lt.)—lieutenant

LZ—helicopter landing zone

magazine—ammunition container

magnesium tears—reference to the substance used in parachute flares

mama-san—any older adult Asian woman; carries pejorative connotation

Mau Than—Year of the Monkey; one of twelve years in the Tet cycle

Med building—medical building

Med-Evac—medical evacuation

Metal No. 8 throat—aluminum tube used for artificial resuscitation

monsoon—tropical rainy season

mortar—short-barreled, high trajectory artillery piece

MP—military police officer

M-16—standard rifle carried by most United States soldiers in Vietnam

napalm—jellied gasoline, usually dropped by aircraft in bombs

North—North Vietnam; formally the Democratic Republic of Vietnam

NVA—North Vietnamese Army, as opposed to Vietcong (VC) or Army of the Republic of Vietnam (ARVN)

O Club—officers' club; bar for military officers

O.D.—Olive drab

Officers' Open Mess—dining facility for military officers

105—105-millimeter artillery

155—155-millimeter artillery

P—piastre; South Vietnamese money

Pentax—brand name for a camera

Pearl of the Orient—Saigon

PFC—private first class

Plain of Jars—geographical area in Laos

point, point man—lead person on a patrol

punji stake—type of nonexploding boobytrap; sharpened bamboo stick, often smeared with human or animal excrement

quad .50—four .50-calibre machineguns, usually truck mounted

quonset hut—cheap, easily constructed permanent structure used by the military for barracks, hospitals and other purposes *rach*—river

ROTC—Reserve Officers Training Corps

round—one unit of ammunition; a bullet or artillery projectile

Round Eyes—Americans

Saigon tea—high-priced nonalcoholic drink served in bars catering to United States servicemen; when a GI bought a bargirl a drink, the bartender would serve the woman Saigon tea instead of alcohol

salty dog—Appalachian folksong with sexual connotations

sapper—demolitions expert

satchel charge—explosive device

search-and-destroy—type of infantry operation

shrapnel—metal fragments from any explosive device

slickship—troop-carrying helicopter

starlight scope—infrared device for enhancing night vision

Tan Son Nhut—main airbase serving Saigon

TC—tracked vehicle commander

Tet—Lunar New Year

ti ti—a little

track—tracked vehicle such as a tank or armored personnel carrier

Trinh—Trinh Cong Son; popular Vietnamese folksinger of the 1960s and 1970s

To Do Street—main bar and prostitution district of Saigon

2, 4, 5-T—components of the chemical defoliant commonly known as Agent Orange, a substance now widely believed to be carcinogenic

Udorn—airbase in Thailand used by United States forces during the Vietnam War

U Minh Forest—Viet Cong stronghold not far from Saigon

utility jacket—part of a Marine work uniform; the army called the same uniform *fatigues*

VC—see Viet Cong

VD—venereal disease

Victor Charlie—military phonetic alphabet for VC; see Viet Cong

Viet Cong—Vietnamese communist; guerrilla forces and political cadre fighting the United States-backed government of South Vietnam; military arm of the National Front for the Liberation of Vietnam, founded 1960; the distinction between Viet Cong and North Vietnamese Army is often blurred

vox populi—Latin for "voice of the people"

Zippo—type of cigarette lighter

RECOMMENDED FOR FURTHER READING
A SELECTED BIBLIOGRAPHY BY JOHN CLARK PRATT

(NOTE—Because the facts of the Vietnam War often seem so contradictory and confusing, I suggest that what the war was really all about cannot be understood by ignoring the fiction, poetry, and drama written about it. Accordingly, this bibliography is designed for the reader who wants primarily to experience the human dimension of the Vietnam War.)

GENERAL WORKS

Harrison, James Pinckney. *The Endless War: Vietnam's Struggle for Independence.* New York: McGraw-Hill, 1982. Scholarly examination of the intentions of Vietnam during its revolutionary century. One of the few dispassionate books that shows the failure of American policy and the reasons for the North Vietnamese success.

Karnow, Stanley, *Vietnam: A History.* New York: Penguin, 1984. A companion to the PBS TV series, this book is less a history than it is the overview of a journalist. Provides an acceptable gloss of the Vietnam portion of the war (Laos and Cambodia are ignored). Numerous factual oversights.

Lomperis, Timothy J. *The War Everyone Lost—and Won.* Baton Rouge: Louisiana State University Press, 1984. Takes all sides to task for failed policies, and by showing how results so often defy intentions, shows how the war began, developed, and ended almost in spite of design and strategy.

MacLear, Michael. *The Ten Thousand Day War.* New York: St Martin's Press, 1981. An often phrenetic gloss, but filled with information. This book is an expanded version of the shooting script for the TV series of the same name.

Pratt, John Clark. *Vietnam Voices: Perspectives on the War Years, 1941-82.* New York: Penguin, 1984. An introductory collage containing chronologically arranged excerpts from all writings by all sides: documents, poetry, memoirs, letters, audiotapes, graffiti, fiction, etc. This book is *not* an anthology but is designed to show the whole war by the words of those who planned, designed, conducted, protested against, and fought it.

Terry, Wallace. *Bloods: An Oral History of the Vietnam War by Black Veterans.* New York: Ballantine, 1985. The most complete treatment of the black soldier's experience in Vietnam—and afterward. Shows the feelings of blacks toward whites as well as toward their Asian foes by means of carefully edited interviews.

VIETNAMESE VOICES

Bui Diem. *In the Jaws of History.* Boston: Houghton Mifflin Co., 1987. Former South Vietnamese Ambassador to the United States details from his point of view the effect of American politics on his country's defeat. This book has been denounced and praised by both sides—and contains a great deal of detailed information about intergovernmental relations throughout the war.

Tran Van Don. *Our Endless War.* Novato, Calif.: Presidio Press, 1978. Former high-ranking South Vietnamese military officer speaks with some bitterness about his country's becoming aligned with foreign powers, especially the United States. A fascinating, but extremely partisan view.

Truong Nhu Tang. *A Vietcong Memoir.* San Diego, Calif.: Harcourt, Brace, Jovanovich, 1985. A founder of the National Liberation Front, Tang worked undercover as a high official of the South Vietnamese Government and upon Saigon's collapse, was appointed Minister of Justice in the Communist regime. His book claims that the original revolution was subverted by the North, forcing Tang and other Viet Cong into exile. Emphasizes the naïveté of the Americans.

MEMOIRS

Broughton, Jack. *Going Downtown: The War Against Hanoi and Washington.* New York: Orion Books, 1988. Author of *Thud Ridge* (1969) details the life of a fighter pilot flying missions in the North. Excellent insight into the mechanization and politicization of a high-tech air campaign.

Caputo, Philip. *A Rumor of War.* New York: Holt, Rinehart & Winston, 1977. As a Marine officer (1965) and a correspondent (1975) in Vietnam, the author brings a wide-ranging perspective to the entire war.

Ehrhart, W. D. *Vietnam-Perkasie.* Jefferson, N.C.: McFarland, 1983. The first of a trilogy (the others are *Passing Time* and *Going Back*), this book shows poignantly how a young, patriotic Marine lives a disillusioning lifetime in one year in Vietnam. One of the most honest books about the war.

Herr, Michael. *Dispatches.* New York: Alfred A. Knopf, 1977. Brilliantly written, eclectic, stylized series of impressions by a correspondent.

Mason, Robert. *Chickenhawk.* New York: The Viking Press, 1983. Detailed story of a helicopter pilot's training and combat experience.

O'Brien, Tim. *If I Die in A Combat Zone*. New York: Dell/Laurel, 1979. The best written narrative of a young man's Army experiences in the war.

FICTION

(NOTE:—The books that follow have been arranged by approximate *internal* chronology; that is, the events of each novel take place during the time period identified in the left-hand brackets. The Act divisions follow the format of *Vietnam Voices*, where the war is broken into sections that follow obviously major turning points, which are identified briefly below. Anyone who reads these novels in the order indicated should have a fine understanding of almost all phases of the war—except the air war in the North and the prisoner-of-war experience. Good, accurate fiction about these two subjects has yet to be published.)

Prologue—to 1955, the accession of Premier Ngo Dinh Diem.

[1948-54]   Meiring, Desmond. *The Brinkman*. Boston: Houghton Mifflin, 1965. French occupation and defeat in Vietnam.
[1951-52]   Greene, Graham. *The Quiet American*. New York: Penguin, 1962. First American covert presence.
[1954]   Bosse, M. J. *The Journey of Tao Kim Nam*. New York: Doubleday, 1959. North Vietnamese boy elects to live in South.
[1954-55]   Larteguy, Jean. *Yellow Fever*. New York: E. P. Dutton, 1975. Evacuation of Hanoi. U.S. helps install South Vietnamese President.

Act I—1955-1963, to the murder of President Diem and the assassination of JFK.

[1960-61]   Baber, Asa. *The Land of A Million Elephants*. New York: Morrow, 1970. Laos. The American presence and Kong Le coup.
[1962]   Halberstam, David. *One Very Hot Day*. Boston: Houghton Mifflin, 1967. American advisor assists South Vietnamese regular troops.
[1962-63]   Crumley, James. *One To Count Cadence*. New York: Random House, 1979. First American Army units sent in civilian clothes.

[1962-63]   Sanders, Pamela. *Miranda*. Boston: Little, Brown, 1978.
            Female news stringer covers the war in Laos and
            Vietnam.
[1963]   Hempstone, Smith. *A Tract of Time*. Boston: Houghton
            Mifflin, 1966. CIA advisor to Montagnard forces.
            Diem coup.
[1963]   Larson, Charles. *The Chinese Game*. Philadelphia:
            Lippincott, 1969. U.S. Army advisor with Montag-
            nards. Diem coup.
[1963]   Vaughn, Robert. *The Valkyrie Mandate*. New York:
            Simon & Schuster, 1974. U.S. Senior Military
            Advisor with Vietnamese. Diem coup.
[1963]   Dinh, Tran Van. *No Passenger on The River*. Ft.
            Collins, Colo.: Pratt, 1988. Vietnamese officer and an
            American woman. Diem coup.

Act II—1963-68, to the North Vietnamese "Tet" Offensive.

[1964]   Ford, Daniel. *Incident at Muc Wa*. New York:
            Doubleday, 1967. Army Special Forces advisor at
            outpost.
[1964]   Moore, Robin. *The Green Berets*. New York: Crown,
            1965. Army Special Forces advisors with larger units.
[1964]   Kaiko, Takeshi. *Into A Black Sun*. New York:
            Kodansha, 1980. Japanese newsman with U.S.-
            advised South Vietnamese rangers.
[1964]   Stone, Scott. *The Coasts of War*. New York: Pyramid.
            1966. U.S. Navy-advised junk fleet in action.
[1965]   Shea, Dick. *Vietnam Simply*. Coronado, Calif.: Pro
            Tem, 1967. Verse novel. U.S. Marines land in
            Vietnam.
[1966-67]   Smith, Steven. *American Boys*. New York: G. P.
            Putnam's Sons, 1975. U.S. Army Airmobile unit in
            action.
[1966-67]   Pelfrey, William. *The Big V*. New York: Liveright, 1972.
            U.S. regular army units experience the war.
[1967-68]   Heinemann, Larry. *Close Quarters*. New York: Farrar,
            Straus, & Giroux, 1977. U.S. Armored Cavalry in
            combat in Tay Ninh Province.
[1967-68]   Roth, Robert. *Sand in the Wind*. Boston: Little, Brown,
            1973. U.S. Marine infantry combat novel. Tet
            offensive.

[1967-68]   Hasford, Gustav. *The Short-Timers.* New York: Harper & Row, 1979. U.S. Marines at Hue during Tet offensive.

[1967-68]   Heinemann, Larry. *Paco's Story.* New York: Farrar, Straus & Giroux, 1986. Wounded soldier returns home to Midwest.

[1967-68]   Currey, Richard, *Fatal Light.* New York: E. P. Dutton, 1988. Sensitive story of Army medic at war and at home.

Act III—1968-70, to the Kent State shootings.

[1968]   Bunting, Josiah. *The Lionheads.* New York: George Braziller, 1972. U.S. Army in Delta and at Headquarters.

[1969]   Huggett, William T. *Body Count.* New York: G. P. Putnam's Sons, 1973. U.S. Marines at Khe Sanh and elsewhere.

[1969-70]   Pratt, John Clark. *The Laotian Fragments.* New York: Avon, 1985. Air war in Laos fought by Forward Air Controllers.

[1969-70]   Wright, Stephen. *Meditations in Green.* New York: Scribner's, 1983. Army soldiers at war and at home.

[1969-70]   Fuller, Jack. *Fragments.* New York: Morrow, 1984. Army action. Problems upon returning home.

[1970]   McQuinn, Donald. *Targets.* New York: MacMillan, 1980. MACV Headquarters, Saigon. War is being lost.

Act IV—1970-73, to the truce agreement.

[1970-71]   Suddick, Tom. *A Few Good Men.* New York: Avon, 1978. U.S. Marines in action as the war winds down.

[1971-72]   Del Vecchio, John. *The Thirteenth Valley.* New York: Bantam, 1982. Microcosm of U.S. Army in Vietnam.

[1973]   Stone, Robert. *Dog Soldiers.* Boston: Houghton-Mifflin, 1974. U.S. setting. Veterans smuggling dope.

Act V—1973-75, to the occupation of Saigon by the North Vietnamese.

[1973-74]   Brooke, Dinah. *Games of Love and War.* London: Jonathan Cape, 1976. All services. Action in Laos and Saigon.

[1975]   Kalb, Bernard and Marvin. *The Last Ambassador.*
           Boston: Little, Brown, 1981. State Department and
           Army personnel and the fall of Saigon.
[1975]   Harper, Stephen. *Live Till Tomorrow.* Ft. Collins,
           Colo.: Pratt, 1989. The fall and evacuation of Saigon.

OTHER FICTION

[1968-71] Webb, James. *Fields of Fire.* Englewood Cliffs, N.J.:
           Prentice-Hall, 1978. Traces members of a Marine unit
           through combat and return.
[1950s to Fleming, Thomas, *Officers' Wives.* New York: Double-
1970s]   day, 1981. Panoramic study of West Point graduates
           and their wives.
[Future]   Haldemann, Joe. *The Forever War.* New York: Ballan-
           tine, 1976. Science Fiction. A war in space much like
           the war in Vietnam.
[Future]   Winn, David. *Gangland.* New York: Alfred A. Knopf,
           1982. Satirical novel set in Vietnam and California.
[Future]   Rinaldi, Nicholas. *Bridge Fall Down.* New York: St.
           Martins / Marek, 1985. What if the war had continued
           into the 1980s?

DRAMA

Coming To Terms: American Plays and The Vietnam War. New
York: Theatre Communications Group, 1985. Anthology of short
plays.
Garson, Barbara, *MacBird.* New York: Grove, 1967. Satire of
President Johnson and Secretary McNamara.
Gray, Amlin. *How I Got That Story.* New York: Dramatists Play
Service, 1981. Study of the problems in learning the truth about
the war.
Rabe, David. *The Basic Training of Pavlo Hummel/Sticks and
Bones.* New York: Penguin, 1978. Two plays about war-related
stresses and issues.

LITERARY CRITICISM

Beidler, Philip D. *American Literature and The Experience of
Vietnam.* Athens: University of Georgia Press, 1982.
Hellmann, John. *American Myth and The Legacy of Vietnam.* New
York: Columbia University Press, 1986.

Lomperis, Timothy and John Clark Pratt. *Reading The Wind: The Literature of the Vietnam War.* Durham, N.C.: Duke University Press, 1987.

Newman, John. *Vietnam War Literature.* 2nd Edition. Metuchen, N.J.: Scarecrow Press, 1988. (Annotated bibliography)

LITERARY ANTHOLOGY

Anisfield, Nancy. *Vietnam Anthology: American War Literature.* Bowling Green, Ohio: Bowling Green University Press, 1987. Novel excerpts, short stories, drama excerpts, poetry.